Memories
of
Cardiff

Part of the
Memories
series

*The Publishers would like to thank the following companies for supporting
the production of this book*

Main Sponsor
Pidgeons of Cardiff

Browning Jones & Morris Limited

Edward England Limited

Evans & Reid Coal Company Limited

Gamlins Music Centre

Graig Shipping plc

Howell's School, Llandaff

MacWhirter Limited

Thayers Ice Cream

First published in Great Britain by True North Books Limited
Units 3 - 5 Heathfield Industrial Park
Elland West Yorkshire
HX5 9AE
Tel. 01422 377977
© Copyright: True North Books Limited 1999

ISBN 1 900463 14 8

*Text, design and origination by True North Books Limited
Printed and bound by The Amadeus Press Limited*

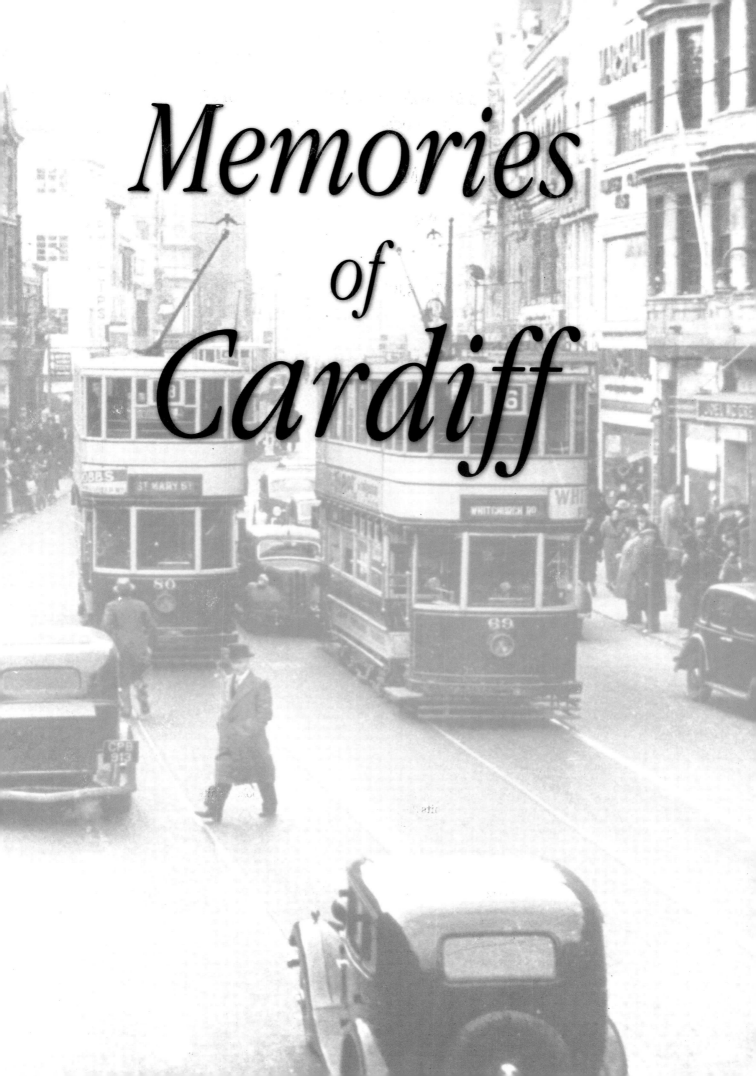

Memories
of
Cardiff

Introduction by Geoff Rich

Memories, said the publisher, give me memories of Cardiff. But a near lifetime of living, loving, laughing and longing in the one community brings more than memories - they weld into attitudes, outlooks, opinions which become in the end, an instinct. That's how it is with me and Cardiff, the town in which I was born, the town where I went to school, failed to master mathematics (two and two can make five if you're an optimist) and have a wonderful twenty years as editor of the *South Wales Echo*.

Memories..... apart from brief safaris to the Valleys where I was evacuated in the Second World War, and to Blackwood (as a teenager reporter), Devon and Reading in pursuit of journalistic expertise, I have lived all my life in Cardiff and surrounds.

When I was 15, attending a night school journalism class, I was asked, "What do you want to be?"

"Foreign Correspondent," I replied with all the staccato crispness of the next Hemingway. I must have been joking; I get homesick at Newport.

Memories are subdivided. Pre-war, war-time, postwar and the rest. The Thirties were dominated by family life in Canton shared with Mother (Maud), Father (George), three brothers and a host of pals from Kitchener Road school, a place of learning certainly, but with no evidence of wealth or easy living. Father was a beacon of strength in a weakening world. He was the last word in hard work. With his right arm blown off at Ypres he forsook the soft option of a clerk's job with the Civil Service after the first world War.

Instead, he went back to his pre-war trade of floor and wall tile fixer. He was magnificent; with sheer perseverance and will-power he kept his wife and four hungry boys. They were the depression years, but for us they were good. Christmas was always

sparkling. The bazaars at Howell's and David Morgan's, with the soldiers that today cost thousands, are still in my mind. In fact, I can still remember the smell of the painted metal soldiers and of the cardboard boxes. They were the days of day trips to Barry Island, sand always in the sandwiches, Whitsun Treats with Bethel Baptist (Mount Stuart Square) to Lavernock?. Long after the war Bethel became a strip club; I was glad my mother never knew...

Then the war, and in spite of an instinctive fear of the swastika appearing on the newsreels in the cinema, an innate belief in the pink bits on the world map which we knew were the British Empire. Came the blitz in January 1941. We were in the Canton Cinema, Rex Harrison was in Night Train to Munich - and an incendiary bomb came through the roof. Home to the Anderson Shelter and a father coming home from work undeterred by the falling bombs. This had nothing on the Western Front, but he never said so.

At school we counted the empty desks and the styes (or wisps as we called them) which were beginning to accumulate on our eyes because of the sleepless nights. Night after night in the shelter. Elder brother Les (who was all of 16) was an A.R.P. messenger. He called in during one raid to see if we were all right. His right trouser leg was missing. "Yes" he said, "And there was five bob in the pocket." We lost him

in an R.A.F raid on Mannheim in March 1945 and none of us has ever stopped missing him.

With the victory came the street parties and a let up for the wonderful mothers who not only held the families together during the vicious war years, but fed us with incredible ingenuity from almost nothing. And all the time so many of them were nursing broken hearts. With the peace came changes. The trams of Cardiff, always a good ride, gave way to trolley buses, which gave way to cars. Yet nothing has worked so well as those trams.

The city centre, relatively unscathed by the blitz, unlike Swansea, Bristol and Plymouth, changed little, but the docks, once the busiest coal-exporting port in the world, died on its derricks. Even the paddle steamers, peddling pleasure throughout the Bristol Channel, went into slow paralysis. But people were glad to be alive and if pleasure came celluloid-wrapped from Hollywood they were happy to share it. I remember six cinemas in the Queen Street area - The Capitol, The Park Hall, The Queen's, The Olympia, The Odeon and The Empire - with queues outside every one of them.

Sport came out of war-time hibernation. Cardiff City had great names - Alf Sherwood, "Buller" Lever, Fred Stansfield, Stan Hollyman, Colin Gibson, "Nobby" Clarke, Billy Reece, and Ernie Carless - but still lost to Moscow Dynamo by 10-1, with a large-nosed winger named Beriah Moore scoring Cardiff's goal. Then the Arms Park claimed my teenage heart with Bleddyn Williams sidestepping his way into

sporting history and many magnificent triumphs including victory over the 1953 All Blacks. So many great names; Jack Matthews, Les Manfield, Cliff Morgan and, bless him, Billy Darch, the scrum half. I never forgave Cardiff RFC for replacing Darch with Haydn Tanner.

Yet Cardiff's greatest claim to international fame was yet to come. The moribund state of Cardiff's docklands had become a scandal since the shipping trade died after the war. Vast spaces became derelict as green fields on the edges of the capital city were swallowed up by development. Then in the 1980s South Glamorgan County Council took an initiative to redevelop the Bute East Dock and this was followed by huge support from the then Secretary of State Nick Edwards who moved the whole concept onto a grander scale. There was conflict, some confusion, a whiff of chaos now and again, but out of it all emerged the Cardiff Bay Development Corporation. I was thrilled as editor of the Echo, to be part of it all. But the rebirth of Cardiff Bay is on the way to becoming reality - to becoming yet another store of memories for the future.

Geoffrey P. Rich.

Geoff Rich OBE

Contents

Around the city centre

With one foot on the tram line, the man near the 'Keep Left' sign was surely fully aware of the oncoming Number 4 tram. Safety rails were a familiar feature of the trams, and this clever innovation would have swept many dogs - and the odd human - away from the tram's wheels, so we have grounds for hoping that this pedestrian did not end up as a part of the city's accident statistics! Readers will remember that Cardiff Corporation ran motor buses and trolley buses at the same time as their fleet of trams. Trams operated in Cardiff for nearly 50 years before they rattled along the rails for the last time in 1950.

This view of Queen Street dates from 1930, and the date is reflected by the ladies' fashions, which changed over the years more often and more quickly than did men's fashions! Behind the knot of shoppers on the pavement on the right, a sign unfamiliar to us today points the way to Woolworth's Sales Room on the first floor of the building. On the opposite side of the road we can pick out the Philharmonic pub and the cinema that would at the time have been the Imperial, though we are more familiar with the establishment after it became the Odeon in 1936.

Left: Trams and buses have long been looked on as very handy mobile advertising hoardings, and the tram travelling along St Mary Street on the left carries an ad that today would raise a few eyebrows. Did any hapless passer-by ever try drinking Typhoo tea as a cure for their indigestion, we have to wonder? And did any of the sufferers get around to asking their doctor about its benefits? Perhaps there may have been some truth in the claim, given the lift that the caffeine would have provided. Be that as it may, advertisers during the 1930s, we suspect, were not required by law to have the same regard for the truth as their modern counterparts. By the 1970s Typhoo had changed their approach to the less contentious 'Join the Tea Set' and 'Typhoo puts the "T" in Britain'.

On the right readers will recognise the ornate canopy over the Queen's Hotel entrance - and will perhaps remember its fate. We can only hope that no luckless client was standing beneath the canopy when it finally collapsed.... The Queen's was AA and RAC registered, and 30 years on was still a smart three-star establishment. In the 1960s bed and breakfast at The Queen's would set you back between £2.5s and £3.5s - a snip at today's prices - until we take into consideration the average weekly wage at the time! The Queens Hotel eventually became the Bank of Ireland.

Above: It was a sunny day in St Mary Street, and it was a good time to fold down the top of your convertible. The motorist on the right has done just that, and is enjoying the spring sunshine. Are he and his passengers about to enjoy afternoon tea at the rather stylish New Dorothy's Cafe nearby, we wonder? Private cars were quite rare during the 1930s in comparison with today, when owning a car (or more than one!) is quite the norm; 60 years ago, cars tended to be owned by the more affluent Cardiffians. On the left, two lady cyclists are also taking advantage of the sunshine; even very close inspection does not make it clear whether they are riding a tandem, or are merely cycling very close together. They are just passing Morgan's chemists shop. In the 1930s, chemists' windows tended to be rather dull compared with those of today, that sparkle with jewellery, hair ornaments, cosmetics and photo-graphic equipment of all kinds. Morgan's was the place to go, however, not only to have your doctor's medicines dispensed but to buy the popular home remedies that had stood the test of time: castor oil, ipecacuanha, Seven Rubbing Oils, camphorated oil, Indian Brandee, Fennings fever powders, Carter's Little Liver pills, pick-me-ups and tonic wines...we could go on and on.

Left: Trams still ran in High Street when this photograph was taken some time during the 1940s, though we have no positive date for the view. It could have been wartime, when due to strict petrol rationing fewer private cars were seen around the city streets. Trolley buses were already beginning to take over from the trams at the time. It would take a very sharp eye to spot the workman working on a street lamp on the right of the road in the far distance, but closer examination reveals that he is doing his maintenance from the top of a very long ladder. No Corporation tower truck for him! Rather nearer, however, on the right, readers will see the canopy over the entrance to Dorothy's Cafe - and remember meeting friends there for coffee or for a very pleasant lunch. On a different note, and taking a trip even further back in time, Cardiff's very first Town Hall once stood in High Street. Built in the mid 14th century, the building housed not only the council chamber but the town gaol, and the meat market, or shambles, was held under cover beneath it. We draw a veil over the smell that must have hung around the place, especially in the heat of summer.... Today, a plaque commemorating the site is mounted on Lloyds Bank in High Street.

Below: This view of St Mary Street was taken from the Wood Street junction looking towards the castle. The banking life of the city is reflected in this stretch of roadway, with Lloyds and Martins as near neighbours on the left. David Morgan's - one of our most popular department stores - is cheerfully hung with flags. Further along on the right readers will recognise the popular indoor market, which still has something for everyone. This photograph dates from 1954 and the market was as popular then as now. The ground floor had an atmosphere of its very own, didn't it? The subtle scents of oranges and apples competing with the sharper odours of onions and leeks.... You could buy more than fruit and vegetables there, however - fish had an entire section (with its own unsubtle odours!) all to itself. Upstairs you could buy anything from a puppy to a Penny Black postage stamp. It was the pet shop, though, that drew the children like flies to a jampot, and the plea 'Can I have one, Mum?' would have come from many a child captivated by a wriggling pup or a cuddly rabbit. Always a firm favourite with children, rabbits have long been regarded as Britain's perfect pet. The stall in Cardiff Market provided the pets - and anything else to do with feeding, rearing, training and even playing with them.

This busy post-war scene of two-way traffic in The Hayes was taken around 1948, when pedestrian-only areas and one-way systems were unknown and largely not needed. A tram rattles by in the foreground, bound for Newport Road, advertising the merits of Merretts. At the time, the Hayes Island was home to the open market - a lively place - and shaded by leafy trees in the right corner of the photograph we can just catch a glimpse of one of the fruit and vegetable stalls. The statue of the controversial philanthropist John Batchelor, Mayor of Cardiff in 1854 and dubbed 'the Friend of Freedom', has gazed down on the busy scene from his plinth for many years, though the man himself is hidden from our view by the trees. The market stalls edged the island, almost enclosing the public loos which have provided for certain needs of passing Cardiffians since Victorian times. The nearby cafe (once the transport

department's parcels office) with its tables beneath the shade of the trees, is the perfect place to sit over a coffee on warm sunny days to watch the world go by.

It is interesting to see a Pickfords van among the vehicles behind the tram, and note that the famous removals firm was still busy around Cardiff in the late 1940s. In the background, the premises of the much-loved department store David Morgan is faced with a framework of scaffolding and long ladders. What work was being carried out there, we wonder?

A glance at the 1930s

HOT OFF THE PRESS

The years of the 1930s saw Adolf Hitler's sickening anti-Jewish campaign echoed in the streets of Britain. On 19th October 1936 Oswald Mosley's 7,000-strong British Union of Fascists clashed head on with thousands of Jews and Communists in London, resulting in 80 people being injured in the ensuing battle. Mosley and his 'blackshirts' later rampaged through the streets beating up Jews and smashing the windows of their businesses.

THE WORLD AT LARGE

In India, Gandhi's peaceful protests against British rule were gathering momentum. The Salt Laws were a great bone of contention: forced to buy salt from the British government, thousands of protestors marched to the salt works, intending to take it over in the name of the Indian people. Policemen and guards attacked the marchers, but not one of them fought back. Gandhi, who earned for himself the name 'Mahatma' - Great Soul - was assassinated in 1948.

ROYAL WATCH

The talking point of the early 1930s was the affair of the Prince of Wales, who later became King Edward VIII, and American divorcee Wallis Simpson. Faced with a choice, Edward gave up his throne for 'the woman I love' and spent the remainder of his life in exile. Many supported him, though they might not have been as keen to do so if they had been aware of his Nazi sympathies, kept strictly under wraps at the time.

It was 1928 when this busy Duke Street scene was caught on camera, and the early view captures crowds of pedestrians but an amazing number of private cars. Motoring was growing out of its infancy at the time, as Britain had seen its first car on the road 34 years earlier, in 1894. By 1930 the number of cars was to soar to over a million. For most ordinary families, however, public transport was good enough, and one of Cardiff's old single-deck trams is making its way along Duke Street. The nearby pub, we note, has Hancocks ales on offer, and the 'Occidental billiard rooms' which occupy an upper floor in the adjoining building add to the rich atmosphere of the view, emphasising

Cardiff's cosmopolitan flavour. Around the corner in Kingsway, Roberts fashion establishment's extensive premises is advertising a new selection of ladies' autumn wear.

Keen-eyed readers will perhaps be able to spot a banner spanning the road in the background. It is advertising Cardiff Flower Show, about to be staged in the Drill Hall. And don't miss the four-legged transport standing at the kerbside on the right, that brings to mind those gentler days when noise from the city's vehicles involved only the rattle of wheels and the clopping of hooves, and the only traffic pollution could be put to good use on the garden!

This lively scene in St Mary Street was snapped some time in the late 1940s, and two clocks in the background agree that the time is 11.10am. The driver in the foreground reminds us of the days when hand signals were part of everyday driving, and though there are few other vehicles actually driving along the road, the kerbsides are lined with parked cars and delivery lorries. Closer inspection reveals that Welsh flags and Union Jacks flap gaily in the breeze from the flagpoles on several offices and stores, leading us to conclude that some special event is being celebrated in the city. As the photograph is unfortunately undated, however, we can offer no suggestion as to what the occasion might have been. The offices of the Western Mail and South Wales Echo and Express can be seen on the left, directly opposite the Sandringham Hotel. Adjoining the Western Mail building is the Queens Hotel, which was both AA and RAC registered.

It seems strange to us today to see vehicles in what is now a pedestrianised area, and although some of us resented the changes to Cardiff's roads when one-way systems, pedestrian streets and brand new ring roads were first introduced, we can today appreciate the difference in our shopping streets. Motorists, meanwhile, have grown used to the 'Alice through the Looking Glass' approach to motoring (head off in the opposite direction to your destination), which seems to work well most of the time.

Both pictures: Isn't it amazing how familiarity can breed, if not contempt, at least inattention? Passers-by in Duke Street are so used to seeing Cardiff Castle that they rarely if ever stop to admire the majestic beauty of the building, which has around 2,000 years of history that goes back to the days when the Romans built a fort here in the first century AD. Until the early 1920s a row of old properties stood in front of the castle walls. Their demolition in 1923-24 gave us the green lawns and open view of the castle that we appreciate today. It was a pleasant sunny day when the early 1950s scene was captured from the clock tower of the castle (above), and the sun blinds are down above Burtons windows to protect their display from the glare. Montague Burton's good quality menswear has been a firm favourite with gentlemen for many years, and virtually every town and city in Britain has at least one branch. The story goes that when soldiers were demobbed they were given vouchers to be outfitted at Burtons. They went along to the nearest branch and were kitted out in what was termed 'the full Monty' - a phrase which has come to mean something rather different! A decade on, the scene has changed little apart from the design of the cars; this second view (left) dates from 1962. In the intervening decade, car designers gave us a longer, sleeker shape and lighter colours, though there were still a number of the old 'sit up and beg' vehicles around...is that an old Ford Popular near the end of High Street? We can see that Burton's has in the meantime had a facelift, giving the store a smart new frontage, and further along, the entrance to Duke Street Arcade can perhaps be picked out. We can count ourselves privileged to have retained our characterful arcades when many cities lost so much of their Victorian heritage during the nation-wide drive for 'regeneration' during the 1960s and 70s.

Cardiff's open spaces bring a breath of fresh air to the city centre

Spread out below like a three-dimensional map, this view of the city centre is a reminder to those who lived through all the changes of the 1960s and 70s, of Cardiff as it used to be. The photograph is dated 3rd August 1950, and from this height we can pick out many familiar landmarks. With the Central Station on the left, the railway line crosses the foreground, carrying the eye towards the gas works on the right, now gone from the scene. Cardiff Arms Park juts into the picture on the left, while not too far away St Mary Street leads up towards the castle. Cardiff is fortunate in having so much open space right in the city centre; readers will perhaps remember the pavilion that was built in Sophia Gardens the year after the photograph was taken - sadly short-lived, as heavy snowfall on its flat roof eventually put paid to the structure. Arranged in a stylish row and built around the turn of the century, the Law Courts, City Hall and the National Museum are easily picked out, with University College (before the extensions were added) to the rear of the museum. It seems strange to see our city without the modern shopping centres and multi-storey car parks that have been added in recent years, along with the Boulevard de Nantes, skirting north of Cardiff's shopping centre, and the widened Bute Terrace and Adam Street to the south.

St John's church clock informs us that the time is 4.58, and in Church Street only a few stragglers are left hovering around the shops. Around the city, offices would be closing, shops would be pulling down their blinds and another teatime rush would begin. The photograph dates from the late 1940s, when Cardiff was drawing breath and recovering from the dire effects of World War II. The church's history goes back much further than that, however; incredibly this tower, designed by John Hart, dates from the 15th century, and is widely recognised as a very fine example of medieval architecture.

Note the interesting sign outside the butcher's shop on the left of Church Street, which informs passers-by that this establishment sells best Welsh meat only. There was a time when small butchers such as this one were a common sight around Cardiff. Sadly, many of them are gone, together with the personal service we once took for granted. Small grocery chains and corner butchers were the traditional way to shop, and customers would queue to be served while the butcher cubed our stewing steak and cut our sausages from a long string hanging over the counter. A far cry from today's plastic packs! People might have had to wait a while longer to be served, but at least they had the benefit of personal attention from the staff.

Below: A cat's cradle of overhead wires hangs low overhead in this 1946 view, and tram and trolley bus travel together along Castle Street, reminding us that the two traffic systems existed side by side at the time. Readers who can remember Cardiff's uncomfortable and draughty trams will perhaps still have a soft spot for them. Even at the beginning of the 1940s, however, the tramway had seen better days, and when this image was captured for posterity the days of Cardiff's ageing trams were very definitely numbered and had limited time left to them. Trolley buses had begun to replace the trams between 1941 and 1943, and eventually the last of the trams were taken out of service and sent on their way to that great tram shed in the sky.

It is interesting to note that the police officer on point duty in the photograph is not wearing the usual bobby's helmet. But with or without it, he was performing a valuable service in keeping Cardiff's traffic running smoothly. There was a time when every major junction in every major town had its traffic 'bobby'; remember those black and white zebra-striped boxes they used to use? But one by one they departed, leaving motorists with a legacy of traffic lights to contend with at each junction. Traffic lights, while no doubt keeping the traffic flowing smoothly through the town centre (in theory at least), somehow lack the personal touch provided by the good old British bobby.

Bottom: The tower of St John's church is the vantage point for this bird's eye view of the city centre as it was in 1954, and the camera shot takes in a huge crane that dwarfs the surrounding tall buildings. The work in progress was the building of the new British Home Stores on the site of the old Carlton Restaurant. The Carlton was at one time a favourite venue for an evening out in Cardiff, and after a superb meal in the restaurant pleasure seekers could go on to spend an enjoyable few hours in the ballroom, circling the floor to their favourite tunes. In 1941, German bombs interrupted the waltzes, foxtrots and quicksteps; the Carlton was badly damaged in one of the bombing raids that devastated the city, and from then on, only the frontage of the building remained in use. The Carlton was demolished in 1954 to make way for BHS, which has become one of Cardiff's more popular stores.

A sight that takes visitors' breath away as they drive along the Boulevard de Nantes (built after this photograph was taken) on their first trip to Cardiff is that of the municipal buildings, which can just be seen in the background of this view. Built of sparkling white Portland stone, the trio of beautiful buildings - the Law Courts (on the far left), the City Hall, and the National Museum of Wales - create an elegant atmosphere that compare favourably to anything Europe can offer.

How many readers remember the parrot that once lived on an upper floor of the Terminus pub in St Mary Street? A source of amusement to locals who were used to hearing the comments of the talkative bird as they made their way to the Penarth bus stop outside the door of the pub - and a cause of puzzlement to strangers walking by, who found themselves the target of the parrot's less than polite comments - all delivered, of course, in a perfect Cardiff accent! How many of them wondered whether some modern-day Mrs Rochester had been locked up to go mad in that upper room? Parrots are long-lived, and for all we know, this pet Polly may live on somewhere in Cardiff, still giving passers-by a chuckle... This photograph

A glance at the 1930s

MELODY MAKERS
Throughout the 1930s a young American trombonist called Glenn Miller was making his mark in the world of music. By 1939 the Glenn Miller sound was a clear leader in the field; his clean-cut, meticulously executed arrangements of numbers such as 'A String of Pearls' and 'Moonlight Serenade' brought him fame across the world as a big-band leader. During a flight to England from Paris in 1944 Miller's plane disappeared; no wreckage was ever found.

GETTING AROUND
At the beginning of the decade many believed that the airship was the transport of the future. The R101 airship, however, loaded with thousands of cubic metres of hydrogen, crashed in France on its maiden flight in 1930. Forty-eight passengers and crew lost their lives. In 1937 the Hindenburg burst into flames - the entire disaster caught on camera and described by a distraught reporter. The days of the airship were numbered.

SCIENCE AND DISCOVERY
By observing the heavens, astronomers had long believed that there in the constellation of Gemini lay a new planet, so far undiscovered. They began to search for the elusive planet, and a special astronomical camera was built for the purpose. The planet Pluto was discovered by amateur astronomer Clyde Tombaugh in 1930, less than a year later.

dates from 1985, and even though St Mary Street was far from congested with traffic at the time, a cyclist is making himself extremely unpopular with the driver of the car following closely behind by hogging the middle of the carriageway. Since then, the safety of cyclists, as well as the benefits of bike riding, has become an issue, with the establishing of cycle lanes and the wearing of safety helmets encouraged.

Above: Framework of scaffolding surrounds another of Cardiff's old properties that is being demolished for redevelopment. Howells sweets and tobacco shop in Wharton Street is nearest the camera, while E H Bowcott Ltd Pork Butchers next door was a regular port of call for many of the housewives of Cardiff. Cross Brothers ironmongers can be seen in the distance; the building was eventually to make way for St David's Hall.

The old library in Trinity Street takes up much of the background, and whether you wanted to unwind with one of Miss Read's Village books, or maybe preferred something a little more humorous, such as Monica Dickens or P G Wodehouse, or enjoyed the edge-of-the-seat excitement of Agatha Christie or Edgar Wallace, there was something in the library to suit your taste in fiction. A huge selection of non-fiction would give you information about wide-ranging topics, while records and tapes were on loan to those who felt like relaxing in front of the fire with Tchaikovsky, Louis Armstrong or Jimi Hendrix. The central library was opened in two stages, in 1882 and 1896, and the facility was well used by Cardiffians for more than a century. The new County Library opened in Frederick Street in December 1988, adding an exciting modern development to Cardiff's rich culture.

This page and facing page bottom: This was Kingsway in the late 1950s - not quite traffic free, but certainly not bumper-to-bumper! In the not too distant future, this stretch of roadway would become part of the ring road that keeps much of the heavier traffic away from the city centre, passing the castle and continuing on to join with the elegant sweep of the Boulevard de Nantes.

The Rose and Crown on the left of Kingsway will evoke many memories of years gone by; how many readers will admit to enjoying their very first drink there in the days of their youth? The old pub is still the favourite watering hole of many Cardiffians, though in company with most older pubs the building has been refurbished to keep up with modern trends. At least it has not been given one of those oh-so-trendy names like The Rat and Parrot or the Fates and Firkin! To the left and behind the Rose and Crown, the stately tower of St John's church stands sentinel over the quiet scene. A few pedestrians are crossing the bridge where the pedestrian subway is today. In ancient times this bridge spanned the moat which went on to become the Glamorgan Canal. The buildings to the right of the photograph are in Duke Street; spot the half-timbered Rummer Tavern squashed between the adjoining buildings like some exotic sandwich filling. The ground floor of the premises to the left of the Rummer Tavern housed Techniquest before the innovative science discovery centre made the move down to the Bay.

Many readers will remember Kingsway Garage (E R Forse Ltd), (below left) whose fleet of coaches and limousines were a familiar sight around the city. Many were the trips to Barry Island, Porthcawl, Ross on Wye, the Brecon Beacons and even further afield that were taken in a Forse's coach! E R Forse was also a filling station, and those who were drivers in the 1950s and 60s will no doubt have filled their tanks there on many occasions.

The residential part of Cardiff Castle can just be seen behind the trees in this early 1960s view of the same stretch of Kingsway (bottom). Once the home of the Bute family, who rebuilt the castle in the late 19th century on the site of the original Norman and Roman structures, Cardiff Castle was handed to the City of Cardiff in September 1947.

It would cause us some concern today to notice that the driver of the Morris Traveller parked on the left of Frederick Street has left his door open. Is the gentleman nearby, wearing a hat, the absent-minded owner? Or does the car perhaps belong to the photographer who had nipped out for a minute to snap this scene? Long lines of parked cars on both sides of the road remind us that the parking restrictions imposed by double yellow lines were not in force here. The premises of the Associated Wholesale Stationers was in Raebur House, which at one time was the newsroom of the Cardiff City Library. Further along were the Revo Electric Company and Squirrell's, though the name of the little tobacconist escapes us; the Rover dealer occupied the white building in the background, more than likely accounting for the number of vehicles parked nearby.

Frederick Street has lived through many changes in its lifetime. During the early part of the 19th century the cattle market was situated where the new library stands today. The street also boasted a number of large and stylish houses - the homes of prominent and well-to-do Cardiffians, to be replaced in later years by rows of more modest houses. This particular view of Frederick Street dates from the early 1950s - and even more drastic changes were on the far horizon.

ately spot the lovely old Morris Minor, interestingly the first all-British car to sell more than one million. Developed by designer Alexander Issigonis, who also gave us the Mini, this tough little car has remained popular and is today attracting quite a following. Updating the Minor to keep pace with modern day traffic has become advisable, and work that involves adding modern disc brakes and updated suspension is now being carried out in specialist classic car centres around the country.

Above: A nostalgic view of Churchill Way that will call up a few memories among our readers, though this row of houses, and the community of families who made their homes there, has now passed into the history books. Off picture to the right lies the Welsh Calvinistic Methodist Chapel, which today is home to an architect's office.
And what a wealth of memories this row of vehicles stirs up! All were familiar around our city during the early 1960s (this photograph dates from 1962). The Italian styled Austin A40 in the foreground, for example, will be no doubt have been the first car owned by more than one reader. Parked next in line is a two-tone Triumph Herald, well-known for its tight turning circle, which was so good that it formed part of the car's advertising campaign - and those 'ban the bomb' type tail lights distinguish the light-coloured Mark 1 Ford Cortina nearby. Classic car enthusiasts will immedi-

Top: We seldom see smaller filling stations like the Taff Garage Co, motor engineers, but back in 1962, the year of the photograph, they seemed as common as those large ones with six or nine petrol pumps are today. Car valeting was among the services offered by this facility. Remember Shell's jolly little TV jingle that was around at the time? 'Keep going well, keep going Shell -' Readers could probably sing it now if hard pushed, though they would probably prefer not to.... With the Roman Catholic church hall to our left and Bute Street behind us, this view of David Street looks northwards towards Bridge Street. We can surmise from the Winstone lorry parked at the kerbside, and the ladders it carries, that one of these properties on the right is about to undergo a few repairs to its roof - though the only workman in evidence is still contemplating the unloading of the equipment. Winstone were well-known local builders, thought to have been based in Canton at the time.

Bottom: Bridge Street in 1962 was a vastly different place from the Bridge Street of today - and not only because of the two-way traffic. We can see that by the early 1960s, traffic was becoming a problem in Cardiff, and only drastic redevelopment of the city centre would keep vehicles flowing smoothly. In spite of the problems, street parking was obviously allowed in Bridge Street at the time, leaving these passing cars and lorry even less space in the relatively narrow road. The cyclist obviously has the right idea, as he can take his bike where no lorry can ever go! Today, he would more than likely be wearing a safety helmet, but back in the 1960s such features were undreamed-of. The group of shoppers on the right have a good deal of choice, from choosing a new three-piece suite or a table and chairs from the Home Furnishing centre to popping into the sweets and tobacco shop on the right for a quarter of mint humbugs. And if they felt hungry after a long day's shopping, a hot Cardiff curry from the Star of India might be just what was needed. Less adventurous souls might have opted instead for cod and chips from the chippy further along.

Right: Who could believe that this was Barrack Lane, as recently as 1962? A row of vans and cars found the narrow cobbled street a convenient parking place on the day this scene was captured for posterity. A sign on the right tells us that this particular property was the premises of Office and Industrial Cleaners; Transport House is in the distance. Today things are very different, and a totally rebuilt Barrack Lane now bustles with market traders in the ultra-modern St David's Market, built in 1987.

Tucked away behind the new library building and with the shopping centre's service ramp curving away upwards nearby, the up to date facility is a favourite with shoppers, who enjoy popping out to the market in their lunch break as well as during special shopping trips into Cardiff. Browsing among the fruit and vegetables is a popular occupation, and uppermost in the minds of shoppers is likely to be the subject of whether to spec out and buy a cauliflower, or to stick with cabbage (cheaper, though perhaps less popular with the kids!) to go with tonight's pork chops.

Down at the docks

A scene to bring back poignant memories to the seamen and dockside workers for whom the docks were not only their daily bread but their daily life. Caught on camera in this 1950s photograph, ships are loading with coal while a tug boat waits on standby to tow the loaded vessels through the lock gates. Pointing skywards in the background is a row of coal tips which would look at home in Mission Control, Houston. These hoists lifted the railway wagons one by one and tipped the contents directly into the hold of the ship.

Lovers of statistics and world records will be inter-ested in the fact that Penarth became holder of the world record in loading by this method. With advance preparations made for the attempt at the record, the ship (whose name, together with the date, has sadly been lost in the mists of time) docked in Penarth on the flood tide; during that day of fast and furious work an incredible 6,000 tons of coal was loaded - and the ship sailed on the same tide when it was on the ebb. As far as we can gather, this record was gained some time in the 1920s, and a few readers may remember hearing about the feat first hand from their justifiably proud fathers or uncles.

Cardiff has seen enormous changes over the last couple of decades, but the greatest transformation of all could be said to be in the waterfront area.

A busy scene of Cardiff's traditional industry - docks, waterways, ships and coal tips - forms a fitting background for the elegant red brick Pier Head building, the offices of the Bute Docks Company. The building was the bold creation of architect William Frame, whose lively imagination endowed the structure with hexagonal chimneys, gargoyles, carved friezes, candle-snuffer pinnacles and a highly ornamented clock tower. A carved panel on the west front of the building bears the arms of the Borough of Bute between a ship and a locomotive, with the fitting motto 'Twy Ddwr a Thân' - 'By Water and Fire'.

The industry that kept the docks alive was to dwindle year by year until no coal passed through Cardiff Docks. Today, however, the waterfront is once more vibrant with life as an incredible seven miles of what was derelict land is transformed into the city's most exciting tourist attraction. Techiquest - a thrilling hands-on centre of science discovery - has huge models and puzzles to amuse and inform adults as well as children; the Atlantic Wharf Leisure Village tempts visitors with a bewildering range of cafes, bars, clubs and restaurants as well as its 26-lane Hollywood Bowl and a 12-screen cinema, and the St Davids Hotel and Spa lists seaweed wraps and massage fountains among its attractions. All proof of Cardiff's ability to 'bounce back'.

Above: A century ago, 'King Coal' reigned in Cardiff, and in the heyday of the docks this kind of scene was a common sight, as hundreds of wagons heaped high with coal from the South Wales collieries waited in sidings for shipment. The wagons, each weighing several tons, were shunted along the docks, where one by one they were hoisted by huge 'coal tips' and emptied directly into the hold of the waiting ships. It was said that the Royal Navy looked on Welsh coal as the best, and that they would use nothing less. The Argentine railways, too, ran on coal imported from Cardiff.

This view was captured in the 1930s, by which time, although Cardiff still led the world as a coal exporting port, trade was already beginning to decrease as ships, trains and industry began to switch to oil. Penarth Dock had ceased operations by the mid 1930s; over the next 30 years trade continued its decline and in 1964 the West Dock closed down. The docks and waterfront continued their slow decay until in the 1990s a bold scheme of regeneration began to turn the waterfront into what was set to become a superb tourist attraction.

At leisure

The Gaumont, where more than a few readers will have spent many happy hours, looks truly the worse for wear in this rather sad photograph. In its heyday the Gaumont was very popular, with children as well as their parents. How many readers belonged to the Gaumont Club? And how many can still remember the club song that was sung at the matinee every Saturday morning? Those were the days.... Flash Gordon, Dan Dare and Superman, and their daring exploits that left the hero in a cliffhanging situation at the end of every episode ('See what happens next week!'), leaving us anxiously wondering about his fate, hoping that our spending money would stretch to a repeat visit the following Saturday. Roy Rogers and his four-legged friend Trigger,

the black-masked Lone Ranger, Abbot and Costello or Laurel and Hardy, were often punctuated by broken film or other projection problems, and breakdowns were accompanied by howls of derision and shouts of 'Put a penny in!'

The Gaumont began life in 1887, when it was Levino's Hall, which was changed a couple of years later to the Empire. In those early days it was a theatre putting on live stage shows, but as early as 1915 it began to show films. It became the Gaumont around 1954, but in the end the old cinema could not compete against television, which had taken off in a big way during the 1950s. Sadly, the end was in sight for the Gaumont, and it was demolished in 1962 to make way for a new C & A store.

'Lullaby of Broadway' was being screened at the Queen's Cinema when this nostalgic photograph was taken in July 1955. The lively 1951 musical starred Doris Day and Gene Nelson. Day, the girl with the golden voice, played a fading actress's talented daughter, who of course went on to become an overnight success. The Queen's unfortunately had a mere three months left to it before the cinema closed in October of the same year. On March 11th 1929, The Queen's made history in Cardiff as the first cinema to screen a full-length talking picture. Back in the 1920s 'talkies' were the wonder technology of the day, and special trains were laid on to bring cinemagoers into Cardiff to hear a singing and talking Al Jolson in 'The Singing Fool'. The film was shown until 4th May, and every day saw well over a thousand seats filled with people who came to shed romantic tears over Jolson's rendering of 'Danny Boy', which became everyone's favourite song.

How many readers remember seeing the very last film to be shown at The Queen's on Saturday, 29th October 1955? 'The African Queen' was one of those 'never to be forgotten' films that live on in our memories, with Katherine Hepburn and Humphrey Bogart playing very memorable parts as a straight-laced missionary and a hard drinking river trader. Great stuff. And if the old Queen's had to go, then 'The African Queen' was the right film to give it a good send-off.

Both pages: Marching smartly into the Arms Park arena in perfect step, this determined group of young athletes (right) were the Welsh competitors in the Sixth British Empire and Commonwealth Games. Each was hoping for victory for him- or herself and for the team. Would any of them come near to matching Roger Bannister's achievement made three years earlier, when he ran what was later dubbed the Mile of the Century in three minutes 59.4 seconds?

The eight-day event was staged in Cardiff in July 1958, and every day the arena virtually bulged with the thousands of spectators who descended on Cardiff. Polo has long been known as one of the royal family's favourite games, and the Duke of Edinburgh captained the Cowdrey Park team in their match at Llandaff Fields. Cowdrey Park won their game against Cirencester Park, and Prince Philip proudly received the Cup from the wife of the Lord Lieutenant, Mrs C Traherne (facing page). The Queen could not attend the closing ceremony that ended the wonderful week of sporting achievements. Instead she sent a recorded speech, and the huge crowd broke into loud cheering as she announced her intention to make Prince Charles the Prince of Wales. A proud moment for our city - and the announcement gave the historic Empire Games an upbeat ending.

The 1950s were key years in British athletics. On 2nd June 1955 Glenn Davis broke the 50 second barrier in the 400m hurdles, while Charles Dumas became the first man ever to clear seven feet in the high jump. During the decade that had passed since the end of World War II sportsmen across the board had fought their way back. The declaration of war on 3rd September 1939 had brought an immediate blanket ban on sport, and many sportsmen and women immediately enlisted in the services. It was Winston Churchill's £50,000 campaign urging the nation to cheerfulness that later gave sport a new lease of life.

This page: The Empire and Commonwealth Games came to Cardiff in 1958, and readers may remember that the months leading up to the mammoth event were packed with frenetic activity in order to get everything ready in time. These photographs were taken in March 1957; although the outer framework was in situ, The Wales Empire Pool, was still under construction and was far from ready for its first competitors! By July 1958, however, all was ready, and thousands of visitors and athletes descended on Cardiff for the week-long extravaganza. The Games were a huge success and were chalked up as a real triumph for Cardiff. The Empire Games swimming pool - which inclined in depth from 3ft to an amazing 16ft - remained one of the city's favourite attractions for many years. It was popular with ordinary swimmers as well as with athletes who used the full-size pool (55 yards long by 20 yards wide) in their training programme. The facility had a lot of extra features that were quite an innovation at the time. Today, of course, restaurants, hot showers, saunas and Turkish baths are more commonly seen in our leisure centres, but 40 years or so ago such amenities were a real talking-point.

The Empire swimming pool became a familiar part of Cardiff life, and stayed with us for exactly 40 years. It was demolished in 1998 as time went full circle and the activity began all over again in the building of the Millennium Stadium in readiness for the 1999 Rugby World Cup. The Cardiff Corporation Transport Department building still stood when these views were shot in 1957, hence the sign that informs us that the speed limit for buses was five miles per hour (below). New transport offices eventually replaced this building in 1973, built on the site of St Dyfrig's church. The wider view (bottom) sets the new facility in context - and the advertising hoardings add their own kind of character to the scene, advising passers-by that Persil washed whiter and that they should enjoy life with Stork margarine. Some of them would perhaps have preferred to enjoy it with Walls ice cream....

Above: Think 'Wales' and you think 'rugby'! Wales have played England in rugby internationals at Cardiff Arms Park since 1893 and in this match, on January 18th 1930, the visiting English were to triumph by eleven points to three. The organisers of the match, the Welsh Rugby Union, warned spectators in advance of 'the possibility of bogus ground admission tickets being sold about the streets or elsewhere.' The warning continued, 'The only official tickets of admission are sold at official boxes situated near the two entrances to the ground, at each of which a police constable will be in charge.' The ground itself was to change in appearance many times during the 20th century. Here, the wooden stand in the background is on the north side of the ground and was demolished three years later and replaced by a much taller structure that was opened when England next played at the Arms Park in 1934. The buildings at the back right of the photograph are the famous Westgate Street flats that still stand today, though they no longer have such a good view of international rugby. In 1930, one of England's players, Harry Rew of Exeter, withdrew injured on the morning of the match and his replacement, Sammy Tucker, was flown across the Channel from Bristol to get to Cardiff in time to play in the match - a very unusual form of transport for amateur sportsmen in the 1930s! The photograph shows the half-time interval when the players stayed on the pitch rather than retired to the seclusion of the dressing room. As the English team suck their oranges, the blazered gentleman on the right (not the coach - unheard of in those days) but a certain Mr H A Haig-Smith, a committeeman of the Rugby Football Union and doubling up as touch-judge, gives them the benefit of his advice.

Below: A sight to stir many memories! Defeats suffered and triumphs gained, bets lost and won, the depths of despair and the heights of euphoria - they were all there at Cardiff Arms Park, along with an entrance fee of just one shilling (5p)! This photograph is unfortunately undated, though we judge that it was taken sometime during the 1930s. Whatever the actual date, however, the picture reminds us of the gentler days when you could leave your bike outside the entrance to the stand (or anywhere else, for that matter), and expect to find it still there when you left the grounds at the end of the match. Cardiff is fortunate in that the stadium was and still is only a stone's throw from the city centre, the bus station and Cardiff Central - great if you had no wheels of your own. A short walk along Quay Street (opposite this entrance) would bring you into St Mary Street.
Once described as 'a cauldron of Celtic fervour', the atmosphere at Arms Park during a home match was a never-to-be-forgotten experience. How many readers joined in the singing, for example, that was part and parcel of every game? Thousands of Welsh voices raised together during the action...marvellous stuff. In our look back with nostalgia at 'the good old days', though, we must be careful not to give any reader the impression that the good times are gone for ever. What about that great victory in June 1999 against South Africa - a great way for the Millennium Stadium (still unfinished at the time) to begin its life!

A glance at the 1940s

HOT OFF THE PRESS

At the end of World War II in 1945 the Allies had their first sight of the unspeakable horrors of the Nazi extermination camps they had only heard of until then. In January, 4,000 emaciated prisoners more dead than alive were liberated by the Russians from Auschwitz in Poland, where three million people, most of them Jews, were murdered. The following year 23 prominent Nazis faced justice at Nuremberg; 12 of them were sentenced to death for crimes against humanity.

THE WORLD AT LARGE

The desert area of Alamogordo in New Mexico was the scene of the first atomic bomb detonation on July 16, 1945. With an explosive power equal to more than 15,000 tons of TNT, the flash could be seen 180 miles away.
President Truman judged that the bomb could secure victory over Japan with far less loss of US lives than a conventional invasion, and on 6th August the first of the new weapons was dropped on Hiroshima. Around 80,000 people died.

ROYAL WATCH

By the end of World War II, the 19-year-old Princess Elizabeth and her distant cousin Lieutenant Philip Mountbatten RN were already in love. The King and Queen approved of Elizabeth's choice of husband, though they realised that she was rather young and had not mixed with many other young men. The couple's wedding on 20th November 1947 was a glittering occasion - the first royal pageantry since before the war.

When push comes to shove, everyone wants to....give Johnny Clay the welcome he deserves! It was 1948, and the talented spin bowler was literally mobbed when he left the train at Cardiff station after Glamorgan won the County Cricket Championship. J C Clay richly deserved the adulation of his fans; never one to ignore an appeal for a helping hand, he had emerged from semi-retirement to rejoin the team and had

crowned the championship by bowling out Surrey and Hampshire, taking the first county title for Glamorgan. Clay had played his first match for Glamorgan in 1921, and by 1924 he had taken over the Glamorgan captaincy - relinquished in 1927 for family and business reasons. His cricketing days, however, were far from over, and he played as often as he was able, establishing himself as one of the best off-spinners in Britain and a force to be reckoned with. After serving as Test selector during 1947-48, J C Clay played county cricket for the last time for Glamorgan in 1949. He served on the county committee, becoming a trustee in 1953 and president in 1960 - a position he held until he died in 1973. A cricketing legend who was sorely missed.

Confidence and professionalism in times of need

Pidgeons, Cardiff's only remaining independent family controlled funeral directors are celebrating their 80th anniversary in the year of the Millennium.

The early days

The company was established in Grangetown by James Pidgeon in 1920, initially as a private car hire firm, during which period they conveyed many celebrities of the times, including King George V (who gave a 10 shilling tip to his driver who happened to be James Pidgeon). Other customers included the American newspaper magnate, William Randolph Hurst, who owned St Donat's Castle, and Joseph Kennedy, father of President John F Kennedy. Pidgeons also supplied cars for wedding hire and charabancs (large open coach-type vehicles) for works outings, Whitsun treats etc.

Pidgeons owned the first motor hearse in Cardiff, which was hired out to undertaking businesses. It was decided by the family at that time that undertaking would be a natural extension to the hire business and during the early 30s Pidgeons conducted their first funeral service.

The founder, James Pidgeon, was born in Lyndhurst, St Canton, and prior to beginning the firm worked on the Taff Valley Railway. He married Kate Eliza Winslade, who was related to the Winslade pop

manufacturers. His son, also named James, and his daughter, Nell, joined him in the business prior to the start of the second world war. His son, James, served in the Merchant Navy as an Engineer Officer worldwide during the war with a brief pause to marry Violet Gale on 16th September 1940. Her father was a docks pilot and she worked at Coastliners.

Facing page, bottom: The founder, James Pidgeon leading a large funeral cortege along Corporation Road, Grangetown. The hearse is a Rolls-Royce.
Below: This picture shows the founder's son, James, chauffering a wedding car outside the Empire Theatre in Queen Street.

Having sustained a broken neck during the war which reduced his height and gave him a characteristic stooped stance, James Pidgeon rejoined his family in the business which went from strength to strength.

Diversification

Gradually Pidgeons reduced their private hire work. In the 1950s they had Cardiff's only purpose built funeral home constructed at 539 Cowbridge Road East, Victoria Park and shortly afterwards decided to dedicate all their considerable experience to funeral directing. The Cowbridge Road building was designed by James Pidgeon senior, who showed considerable foresight in its design and subsequent adaptability for the future needs of the bereaved it was dedicated to serve.

In 1987 James Pidgeon passed away, leaving the future in the hands of his family who still run the company today - his wife, Violet Pidgeon being the Company Secretary and Chairman of the Board of Directors.

The year 1989 saw the premises enlarged to provide enhanced facilities for the bereaved. The chapel, viewing rooms, reception area and arrangement offices are all on the same level so there are no steps for the disabled or elderly to negotiate.

Above: *James Pidgeon outside the rear of Cardiff Railway Station.*
Left: *James Pidgeon (in foreground) awaiting a funeral cortege.*

Wheelchair access is simple, using the gently sloping frontage to the premises.

The entire funeral home is air conditioned, so whatever the weather the

Below: *Wedding cars at Llandaff Cathedral.*

temperature is outside, clients are comfortable when visiting the premises.

The company uses Daimler Limousines which provide plenty of room and comfort for the bereaved and are the finest vehicles available

In the 1950s, Pidgeons had Cardiff's only purpose built funeral home constructed

for the bereaved in Cardiff. The hearses and limousines are the most modern fleet in Cardiff. They are distinguished vehicles and are readily recognised by their distinctive aubergine colour and personalised JP number plates.

Today the dedicated staff at Pidgeons have between them over 300 years of experience in the funereal profession, serving the needs of the bereaved. All the company's funeral directors hold a professional qualification in funeral directing and the remaining staff are highly trained professionals.

When Pidgeons first traded in 1920 there were many undertakers in Cardiff. Times have changed. Today there are no undertakers in Cardiff - funeral directors have taken their place. Many people think undertakers

are the same as funeral directors. This is incorrect - an undertaker will undertake to build you a new wall, or paint your room or even make you a coffee table or undertake your funeral. A funeral director, however, will only provide a funeral or services directly related to it.

Today, Pidgeons is Cardiff's only independent family owned funeral company, being wholly owned by the Pidgeon family since 1920. Pidgeons is run by a local family and employs local staff who are all resident in the local community.

Left: *Daimler hearse and limos travelling along Western Avenue.*
Top: *This picture is believed to have been taken in Wedmore Road and shows some of the company's fleet at that time.*
Below: *The premises and fleet today.*

Events & occasions

Both pages: The 10th of September 1947 was a day of celebration for Cardiff as John Crichton-Stuart, the 5th Marquess of Bute, presented Cardiff Castle and its grounds and Sophia Gardens to the City of Cardiff. Spruced up and wearing their smartest clothes, these children from Cardiff schools wanted to look their very best for the ceremony, and it was a proud moment for their parents when they assembled in front of the castle for the presentation ceremony *(right)*. What a pity that their singing was not recorded! Most of the children in the photograph are carefully following their earnest conductor, and the pianist's page-turner stands at the ready for the moment her services are required - there will be no faltering in this piece of music! And what song were they singing? It was likely to have been 'Hen Wlad fy Nhadau' ('Land of my Fathers'), performed with all the enthusiasm of youthful patriotism. The event was a red-letter day in the city, and great crowds of people flocked into Cardiff centre to watch the ceremony, lining the route of the procession in their thousands *(below)*. The children were given ringside places at the front where they could see everything and feel part of the proceedings. Here the Lord Mayor in his regalia and the civic dignitaries in their formal finery process along Duke Street past the junction with High Street. Cardiff Castle had been in the possession of the Bute family since the 18th century. The Bute fortune was founded on coal, and it was the 2nd Marquess of Bute who established Cardiff as the greatest coal exporting port in the world. The 5th Marquess's generous gift provided Cardiff with acres of unspoiled parkland right in the heart of the city.

Bottom: The date was 27th April 1957, and the elegant towers of Cardiff Castle form a fitting background for what was a significant occasion - the presentation of the freedom of the city to Her Majesty's Welsh Regiment of Foot Guards. The Detachment, with the Regiment's band and drums, presented a fine sight as they assembled on the Castle Green, while assembled on the rostrum were the Duke of Edinburgh (attending the ceremony in his position as Colonel of the Welsh Guards), the Lord Mayor, Alderman D T Williams, and the rest of the Civic party. The bestowal of the Freedom of the City was made in order to officially recognise the achievements and fine record of the regiment, and, of course, to honour the memory of the many who had given their lives during the two world wars.

Sunshine was the bright bonus of the day, and huge crowds watched as Prince Philip and the Lord Mayor inspected the Welsh Guards Detachment, and heard the Town Clerk read the historic resolution of the Council to present them with the Freedom of the City. But everybody loves a parade, especially if there is a rousing band to set the feet tapping, and after the civic presentations in the Lord Mayor's parlour the Duke took the salute as the Detachment marched past the front of the City Hall and through the city centre, where hundreds of Cardiffians young and not so young lined the pavements to watch the procession.

The Freedom of the City gave the Welsh Regiment the right to march through the streets of Cardiff with drums and bands (and fixed bayonets!) on all ceremonial occasions. As today's youngsters would say - cool!

Right: The Silver Jubilee of King George V and Queen Mary was an opportunity for Britons to state their patriotism - and an excuse for a country-wide party. Every town and village made their own plans to deck windows and doorways with red, white and blue garlands, hang bunting across every street and run up the Union Jack from every flagpole. Cardiff put her back into the country-wide party, and held many special events to celebrate the occasion. The photograph shows the illuminated display set up in Park Place to honour the King and Queen.

George Duke of York came to the throne in 1910. The model of the ideal Englishman, King George had made himself immensely popular with his subjects without really trying. He was tolerant of people whose opinions differed from his own - but not afraid to speak his mind when the occasion called for straight talking. Dignified, fair, conscientious and modest, he once remarked on the warmth with which people greeted him during his Silver Jubilee celebrations, 'I am beginning to think they like me for myself.' George V was the first monarch to broadcast a Christmas Day message over the radio; the Christmas Broadcast became the established tradition that we still enjoy today. King George died in 1936; his widow, Queen Mary, lived on until 1953.

Wartime

In 1939 Britain's Prime Minister Neville Chamberlain had made his announcement to the waiting people of Britain that '...this country is at war with Germany.' Cardiff, along with the rest of the country rolled up its sleeves and prepared for the inevitable. This war would be different from other wars. This time planes had the ability to fly further and carry a heavier load, and air raids were fully expected. Air raid shelters were obviously going to be needed, and shelters were built on open places across the town.

By the time war was declared an army of volunteers of both sexes had already been recruited to form an Air Raid Protection service. At first ARP personnel were unpaid volunteers but when war broke out in September 1939 they became paid staff. It was their job to patrol specified areas, making sure that no chinks of light broke the blackout restrictions, checking the safety of local residents, being alert for gas attacks, air raids and unexploded bombs. The exceptional work done by Air Raid Wardens in dealing with incendiaries, giving first aid to the injured, helping to rescue victims from their bombed-out properties, clearing away rubble, and a thousand and one other tasks became legendary; during the second world war nearly as many private citizens were killed as troops - and many of them were the gallant ARP wardens.

At the beginning of the war Sir Anthony Eden, Secretary of State for War, appealed in a radio broadcast for men between 17 and 65 to make up a new force, the Local Defence Volunteers, to guard vulnerable points from possible Nazi attack. Within a very short time the first men were putting their names down. At first the new force had to improvise; there were no weapons to spare and men had to rely on sticks, shotguns handed in by local people, and on sheer determination . Weapons and uniforms did not become available for several months.

In July the Local Defence Volunteers was renamed the Home Guard, and by the following year were a force to be reckoned with. Television programmes such as 'Dad's Army' have unfortunately associated the Home Guard with comedy, but in fact they performed much important work. The Guard posted sentries to watch for possible aircraft or parachute landings at likely spots such as disused aerodromes, golf courses on the outskirts of towns, local parks and racecourses. They manned anti-aircraft rocket guns, liaised with other units and with regular troops, set up communications and organised balloon barrages.

Other preparations were hastily made around the town. Place names and other identifying marks were obliterated to confuse the enemy about exactly where they were. Notices went up everywhere giving good advice to citizens on a number of issues. 'Keep Mum - she's not so dumb' warned people to take care what kind of information they passed on, as the person they were speaking to could be an enemy.

Older folk will remember how difficult it was to find certain items in the shops during the war; combs, soap, cosmetics, hairgrips, elastic, buttons, zips - all were virtually impossible to buy as factories that once produced these items had been turned over to war work. Stockings were in short supply, and resourceful women resorted to colouring their legs with gravy browning or with a mixture of sand and water. Beetroot juice was found to be a good substitute for lipstick.

Clothes rationing was introduced in 1941, and everyone had 66 coupons per year. Eleven coupons would buy a dress, and sixteen were needed for a coat. The number of coupons was later reduced to 40 per person. People were required to save material where they could - ladies' hemlines went up considerably, and skirts were not allowed to have lots of pleats. Some found clever ways around the regulations by using materials that were not rationed. Blackout material could be embroidered and made into blouses or skirts, and dyed sugar sacks were turned into curtains.

Bottom: War had been declared, and every citizen of Britain, young and old, male and female, was called upon to put his or her back into the war effort. Those who did not go into military service of one kind or another worked in factories, dug for victory, gave up their aluminium baths and saucepans, joined organisations and aided in any way they could. These boys from were not going to be left out; they might be too young to fight but while there were sandbags to be filled they were going to do their bit to protect their school building. Thousands of sandbags were used during World War II to protect Cardiff and its beautiful civic buildings.

Right: A proud father poses for the camera with his latest arrival. The baby had not arrived from Mars, in fact the 'arrival' was not a baby at all, but an anti-gas attack suit which was compulsory for babies in the United Kingdom during the second world war. An air pump at the side of the suit enabled anxious parents to replenish the supply of air to the precious package inside. It is said that most babies were less than enthusiastic abut the prospect of being encased in the suit - and who could blame them? The picture was taken in 1939. In the event there was never any gas attack on British soil during the course of the second world war.

No matter what kind of work is in progress, the sight of men working has always attracted passers-by to watch them; dig a hole anywhere, and people will gather to gaze into it!

This particular hole - a trench, in fact - was in Cathays Park, and the year was 1938. That same year, Adolf Hitler signed the Munich Agreement; Britain's Prime Minister, Neville Chamberlain, made the mistake of trusting him, and came home enthusing about 'peace in our time'. Some dubbed Chamberlain the 'Number one World Peacemaker'; fortunately for Britain, however, many others did not have the same trust in Hitler's words, and they continued to prepare for the war that they could see

was looming on the horizon. Protection from air attack was one of the main priorities in an important port such as Cardiff, and work began on digging trenches to give a certain amount of protection in public places around the city. There was no short of work for the unemployed as an incredible nine miles of trenches were dug in Cathays Park (near the Temple of Peace), Sophia Gardens and other open land. The trenches, though, even when roofed over with sheets of corrugated iron, did not offer a great deal of protection - but were at least a step in the right direction. By 1939 war had broken out, and the citizens of Cardiff drew breath and prepared themselves for another long siege.

Both pages: Cardiff suffered horrendous damage during the grim days of the second world war. During 1940 and 1941 death and destruction in the form of high explosives and incendiaries rained down on our city; many public buildings were destroyed, shops and offices in the city centre were fired, and the gas works at Grangetown was badly hit.

It was the ordinary people in ordinary streets of houses, however, who took the full force of Hitler's wrath. Hundreds of homes were totally destroyed, and in the immediate locality slates were blown from roofs and windows were shattered. As the bombs fell fires started up and spread, and no sooner was one fire dealt with than the valiant fire fighters had to move on to the next. Death came without warning to many. It was natural for most people to make their way into the shelters when the sirens sounded. In the outlying areas of Cardiff those who had them went into their Anderson shelters; others not so lucky went down to sit in the cellar or simply crowded together into the space below the staircase - the strongest part of the house.

In Wyverne Road, however, even the Anderson shelter could not save the Palmer family. Some members of the family were in their Anderson shelter, but the result was sadly the same for all, and the entire family - eight children and their parents - were killed. Other people were buried in the wreckage of their own homes. Even after the raids were over there still remained the very real threat from unexploded bombs.

Hundreds of residents in the worst hit areas were evacuated to rest centres - and even there they were not safe. Newport Road was badly hit (facing page, bottom), and steadily falling rain emphasises this bleak scene of homes with missing roofs, bomb craters in the road and a burnt out car. Angus Street suffered during a raid in September 1940 (above), and little was left of some of these homes. In A G Meek's shop on the corner, scarcely a window remained in the entire house and shop. A gentleman in shirt sleeves and waistcoat is philosophically getting on with whatever he could do to get repairs underway - and his action was typical of the average Cardiffian, who simply rolled up his or her sleeves and pitched in. The tales of remarkable heroism in the grimmest of conditions were many, as rescue parties toiled hour after hour in the wreckage of homes and businesses, through fire, water, dust and rubble, to reach bomb victims.

Left: *Readers who are old enough to remember the terrible bombing raids we endured during World War II will also remember the visit of the King and Queen, who came to Cardiff in March 1941 to sympathise with those who had suffered loss of their homes and loved ones during the bombing raids. With their usual warmth and compassion the royal couple chatted with people, listening to the stories of their narrow escapes, their losses and the amazing heroism that characterised ordinary people in those dreadful days. The King and Queen inspected the local Civil Defence units during their tour of South Wales, and left marvelling at the amazing courage of the citizens of Cardiff.*

The royal couple themselves could identify with their people; with their two beautiful daughters they themselves were living and suffering along with the people of Britain through the dark days of war. They showed great courage by staying on in England when they had the opportunity to be evacuated to safety, and earned the respect and admiration of the people by insisting that they be treated like everyone else, even to wartime rationing. The King was almost relieved when Buckingham Palace was bombed. His comment was that he felt he could now identify with his people and look them in the face.

Below: *During World War II buses and trams were not immune from enemy attack, and as their staff were likely to come across the victims of air raids, many were trained to give first aid to people injured by flying glass, falling masonry and in the hundreds of fires that raged around the city. This group of men and women were the Cardiff Transport First Aid Group, who would have done sterling work both on and off duty. The photograph was taken around 1943, and it is interesting to note the uniform of the ladies in the front row, who are likely to have been 'clippies'. Though trousers were becoming more accepted on the fashion scene of the times, their use was still not widespread and many older people tended to be rather scandalised at the sight of a woman wearing what they saw as 'men's clothing'. Trousers, however, were perfectly suited to the job these girls carried out on Cardiff's buses and trams. We can see that one proud father on the back row has brought his little girl along to take part in this group photograph. Who was this toddler - who will now be in her late 50s, no doubt with children and perhaps grandchildren of her own - and what kind of life did she carve out for herself?*

Bottom: Parks and open spaces were the obvious choices as sites for balloon barrages during the second world war, and this demonstration that showed the value of barrage balloons took place in Cathays Park at the beginning of the war in 1939. Watched by a huge crowd of Cardiffians, Civil Defence personnel showed them how the balloons worked and explained their value. Eventually, the Home Guard were largely responsible for organising the balloon barrages. During an air raid the balloons were let loose to fly high over the city, and prevented enemy aircraft from dive-bombing our city streets. It was women who were chiefly responsible for the manufacture of barrage balloons, and theirs was exhausting work. The huge pieces of material would be spread out across the factory floor, and sitting, crouching or kneeling, the women would spend their working day bent low over the balloons. When the manufacture of barrage balloons began at the start of the war, women were not thought to be strong enough to handle the balloons. By 1941 this attitude had changed as womens' talents and abilities were recognised and appreciated. During World War II women replaced men who had been called up for military service, and they worked in many fields that had previously been regarded as 'jobs for the boys'.

Right: Those who have only seen barrage balloons on old wartime photographs will undoubtedly be totally taken aback by the sheer size of these inflatable monsters. Manufactured at the Willows Aircraft Company in Cardiff during World War I, barrage balloons provided a level of protection from air attack. This photograph was taken at the end of the first world war in 1918.

By 1939, advances had been made in aeronautics and planes had the ability to fly further and carry a heavier load; this time, even heavier and more extensive air raids were expected. Parks, recreation grounds, private land, tips, sites cleared for building, and plots of unoccupied land were earmarked as sites for balloon barrages, and within a few hours of the sites being taken over the balloons were in situ. When the air-raid siren sounded, it was time to fly the balloons. When flying high over the city, this ingenious form of defence prevented enemy planes from diving low over the streets to make close-up attacks. Maximum flying height of the barrage balloon was 6,000 ft. Only bad weather prevented the balloons from flying, and on occasions when the sirens sounded in unsuitable weather accidents happened. Sometimes the cables snapped setting the balloon free; frosty nights were a particular problem, as the balloons could ice over and come down.

The Spitfire quickly established itself as an unrivalled fighter

A mechanic does a touch of vital maintenance on Cardiff III, one of the Spitfire aircraft sponsored by Cardiff during World War II. The plane was probably a Spitfire Mark II, with a Rolls Royce Merlin 2 or Merlin 3 engine. The domed cockpit hood was an important modification, as was the bullet proof windscreen which was added in 1940.

When the second world war broke out in 1939, Germany actually had fewer planes than Britain. It would seem that Britain and our allies would therefore have had the advantage; the problem was that at the time our air power consisted of many different types of aircraft, some of which were definitely showing their age. Vickers-Armstrong threw itself into new production in earnest, but manufacture of the Spitfire lagged behind the Hurricane, apparently because of the shape of the wings. By 1940, however, the Spitfire - a high-performance fighter that would have had eight fixed Browning .303 wing-mounted machine guns - entered the war in numbers, and quickly established itself as an interceptor whose performance was unrivalled by any other fighter. With a maximum level speed of 355 miles per hour at 18,500 ft, the Spitfire was capable of climbing 2,300 ft in a minute.

On the move

Above: Paying tolls to get to Cardiff from Penarth and Cogan and back again was always a sore point with drivers who had to stop at the toll gate and dig into their pockets. Motorists have long objected to paying money for the use of roads, bridges and tunnels - and today the ongoing feud with traffic wardens and other authority figures evokes a similar response. Were there as many arguments between the toll-keeper and the driver back then as we see today between motorists and our beleaguered traffic wardens, we wonder? The driver of this lovely old car - thought to be a 1930s Bradford-made Jowett - appears to be paying up without protest, however.

One Penarth resident remembers a Mr and Mrs Trolley, who once lived in the toll-house pictured here; Mr Trolley was the toll keeper at the time, though we cannot put a date to the information. More than a few readers, however, will remember the couple. Older residents might also recall a never to-be-forgotten incident that took place around the time of this photograph. It was during the 1930s that Fred Marsh of Cawnpore Street in Cogan got thoroughly fed up with paying tolls every time he drove over the bridge and into the city centre. Deciding that writing letters was going to get him nowhere, Mr Marsh (so the story goes) decided on an objection with a more pungent bouquet; his protest, calculated to leave a bad smell under the noses of the authorities, involved the placing of a large pile of manure in front of the toll gate. Bring out the shovels, lads, and get ready for a bit of gardening....

Right: It is rush hour in Queen Street, and pedestrians far outnumber vehicles in this 1940s view. Cardiffians want to get home at the end of the day as much as the next person, and after a hard day spent huddled over a typewriter in the office or dealing with awkward customers in the shop, all the average person thinks of is a nice cup of tea, a hot dinner, and an evening spent playing darts down the pub! A couple of jay-walkers take their lives in their hands to cross the busy road in this fascinating view. Note, too the rather nice old 1930s Morris 8 in the foreground, its mudguards and running boards reminding us of a long-past era of motoring - though we have not identified the unfamiliar vehicle in front of it on the left, which carries a trunk behind it. We do recognise the little Ford in the photograph, which looks as though it would like to squeeze through the impossible gap between the Number 2B (or was it 28?) and the Number 16 tram - though the attempt would be doomed to frustration from the outset. It is interesting to note how different was the style of dress a mere 50 years ago, when formal wear with shirts and ties was normal office and shop workwear. Hats were definitely in, and few men would dream of going out without a hat or cap.

How many of us have at some time made our way to Cardiff bus station through the steadily falling rain beneath a dripping umbrella, with wet feet and cold hands? The 'new' bus station was still being built when this rather damp view was captured back in December 1954. Even close examination fails to reveal exactly what these men were moving on their trolley; whatever it was, it was obviously heavy enough to need the muscle power of three hefty workers! The terminal building, which would eventually take up

position on the far left of the photograph, was still little more than a gleam in the architect's eye, and we can see that the construction was in its very early stages. Little action was taking place on this rainy day; are the workers sitting huddled around the stove in their little wooden site hut? And does the hut itself look less than solid? We can surely detect a slight list to starboard - though no doubt it stayed in position long enough to see the building work completed. The real action on this grey day is taking place in the

background, where a row of double-decker buses wait for their passengers to board.

A number of advertising hoardings behind the buses add their own flavour to the scene, informing the travelling public about what was on 'This week at the Pavilion' and advising of the benefits of drinking Guinness. The British public have believed that Guinness was good for them since the drink was first advertised in 1929. Many clever slogans have been produced over the years: remember 'Guinness is Good for you - Just think what Toucan do'?

A glance at the 1940s

MELODY MAKERS
The songs of radio personalities such as Bing Crosby and Vera Lynn were whistled, sung and hummed everywhere during the 1940s. The 'forces' sweetheart' brought hope to war-torn Britain with 'When the Lights go on Again', while the popular crooner's 'White Christmas' is still played around Christmas time even today. Who can forget songs like 'People Will Say we're in Love', and 'Riders in the Sky'?

INVENTION AND TECHNOLOGY
Inspired by quick-drying printers' ink, in 1945 Hungarian journalist Laszlo Biro developed a ballpoint pen which released viscous ink from its own reservoir as the writer moved the pen across the page. An American inventor was working on a similar idea at the same time, but it was Biro's name that stuck. A few years later Baron Bich developed a low cost version of the pen, and the 'Bic' ballpoint went on sale in France in 1953.

SCIENCE AND DISCOVERY
In 1943 Ukrainian-born biochemist Selman Abraham Waksman made a significant discovery. While studying organisms found in soil he discovered an antibiotic (a name Waksman himself coined) which was later found to be the very first effective treatment for tuberculosis. A major killer for thousands of years, even the writings of the ancient Egyptians contain stories of people suffering from tuberculosis. Waksman's development of strep-tomycin brought him the 1952 Nobel Prize for Medicine.

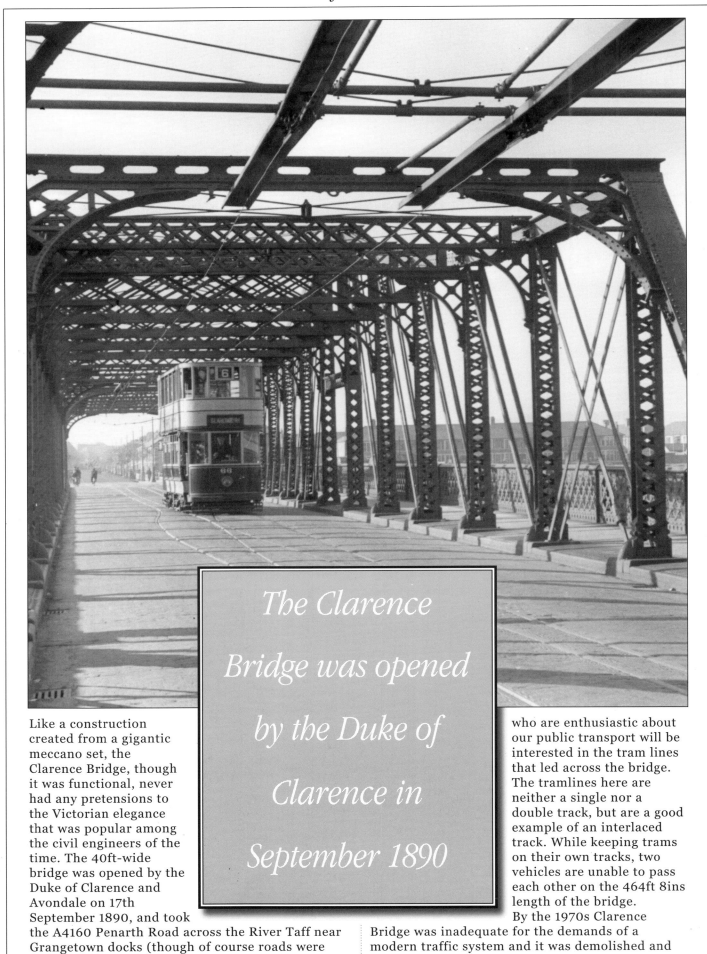

The Clarence Bridge was opened by the Duke of Clarence in September 1890

Like a construction created from a gigantic meccano set, the Clarence Bridge, though it was functional, never had any pretensions to the Victorian elegance that was popular among the civil engineers of the time. The 40ft-wide bridge was opened by the Duke of Clarence and Avondale on 17th September 1890, and took the A4160 Penarth Road across the River Taff near Grangetown docks (though of course roads were not numbered until 1st January 1904). Readers who are enthusiastic about our public transport will be interested in the tram lines that led across the bridge. The tramlines here are neither a single nor a double track, but are a good example of an interlaced track. While keeping trams on their own tracks, two vehicles are unable to pass each other on the 464ft 8ins length of the bridge.

By the 1970s Clarence Bridge was inadequate for the demands of a modern traffic system and it was demolished and replaced by the present bridge in January 1976.

Below: The smart maroon and cream livery of this Rhiwbina bus looks a little dusty, but Bus Number 182 could boast that it had many miles of Cardiff roads behind it! This particular member of the Cardiff Corporation fleet was acquired back in 1938, and it was to see nearly 20 years of service before it was finally withdrawn in November 1957. We have no date for this photograph, but as the bus behind and to the right was a utility vehicle we could hazard a guess that the picture dates from just after World War II.

Cardiff bus operators had a tough time of it during the war. Many of their staff enlisted in the services and women stepped in to replace them where possible. But staffing was far from being the only problem they had to face. Spare parts were like gold dust and were just as elusive, and many of the buses needed urgent maintenance. Yet petrol rationing, coupled with more people commuting to factories, meant that more than ever were using public transport (in 1940 petrol rose to 1/11d a gallon).

The blackout, too, caused problems, and drivers had to learn to 'feel' their way around the city streets, while inside the lights were so dim that the unfortunate conductresses scarcely knew whether they were being given a halfpenny or a shilling.

Bottom: Bus stations and railway stations go together like fish and chips or cheese and wine - but it is surprising how many cities around Britain have separated these two means of transport by a ten or fifteen minute walk. Fine for taxi drivers, though not good for holiday-makers carrying a couple of heavy suitcases and wheeling a baby buggy. Cardiff, however, is different. Travellers arriving by train have only to walk a few yards from Cardiff Central Station to the bus station, from where they can catch a bus home - or indeed travel on to any part of Britain. So sensible! The photograph dates from December 1972, before the bus station received its new facelift, and readers will no doubt remember queuing at these rather draughty stands that gave little protection from the British weather. Taking up the foreground of the picture is the terminal building with its offices and staff canteen. The bus station was modernised in 1983. The sign 'British Rail - Cardiff General' below the station clock leaves us in no doubt of the proximity of the railway station, and visitors from London have long been able to reach Cardiff by train in only a couple of hours. Today, of course, the Channel Tunnel has made the Continent seem nearer than ever before, and travelling from Cardiff to London Waterloo, then on by Eurostar train to Paris, Lille or Brussels, is a simple operation.

A long line of frustrated motorists stretches nose to tail in either direction as they queue to cross the bridge on the A4160 Penarth Road, passing the old toll gate as they go. This was single lane traffic at its deadliest.... But better things lay ahead, and alongside this single span, men and machinery reach out towards each other across the Ely as the fine new bridge takes shape. This fascinating aerial view was taken in 1964, and since that time a series of road building and road widening projects such as Bute Terrace and Adam Street have led to a network of good roads and dual carriageways easing the traffic in the city. Today the new Grangetown Link cuts across the top of this view. Near the bridge the old pump house was still functioning at the time of the photograph; nothing stays the same for ever, though, and while the building is still there it has undergone a change of use in recent years that nevertheless still links it with the past. Seekers after antiques of all kinds can browse here today among the clocks, whatnot stands, china ornaments, washstands (with marble tops if you're lucky) and all the other paraphernalia of days gone by.

Shopping spree

This pigeon's eye view of the CWS water tower in St Mary Street shows us a scene that few ordinary people ever had the chance to see. The marvellous view is probably the last thing on this man's mind, however, as with nerves of steel he mounts the ladder to the very top of the tank to carry out some maintenance job. The photograph was taken back in January 1968; the CWS building is today part of Cardiff's history - though many Co-op stores of course remain around the city.

The Co-operative movement started more than a century ago in Rochdale, where a group of local weavers found 28 people who were willing to pay £1 each to buy goods and open a shop. Customers were awarded a dividend on everything they bought. The idea caught on in a big way, and seven years later the north of England had a total of 130 shops owned by co-operative societies. Eventually there were enough societies to have their own suppliers, the Co-operative Wholesale Society, and beginning with footwear, soap and biscuits the CWS began to manufacture its own goods, provide insurance and arrange affordable funerals. During the earlier years of the 20th Century the Co-op movement was responsible for a vast improvement in the standard of living of the average British working class person.

On a different note, sporting enthusiasts will see the old Cardiff Arms Park stand in the background - today transformed into the Millennium Stadium.

Though this busy scene of High Street is not dated, its atmosphere is that of the 1930s or even 20s. The old trams, the sit up and beg style of car - almost invariably black - and Montague Burtons, which still had its original frontage at the time, set the scene for this journey through the decades. Branches of Burtons around the country always proudly advertised their central London address - 87-89 Oxford Street - on their frontage. Did the man nattily dressed in plus fours just rounding the corner into High Street shop at Burtons for his outfit, we wonder?

Across the road, the Tudor-style pub that we know today as the Goat Major would at that time have been the Bluebell. Spot the sign on the right outside Cooks Tourist Office further along. Today a famous name throughout the world, Thomas Cook, the inventor of the package tour, began his modest travel services in Leicester when he planned local train excursions to nearby beauty spots. Other travel companies existed but Cook was the first to offer a comprehensive service; he personally saw to the train hire and the selling of the tickets, and even took a trip to the holiday destination beforehand to check on the cafes, restaurants and hotels in the area, and the kind of attractions that might interest travellers. He had handbooks printed for each of his passengers, listing the landmarks to look out for along the route, and even went along on each trip to make sure things ran smoothly.

The well-stocked fruit stalls of the open market in Mill Lane would have made a good starting place for a lot of Cardiffian housewives, who week after week would catch a bus into town and tour the market to find the best - and cheapest - apples, pears, oranges, grapefruit and bananas. Buying tomatoes and gibbons from one stall, apples and sprouts from another and perhaps potatoes and a couple of grapefruit from a third have always been part of the fun of bargain hunting in the market. The prices charged by markets and street traders have traditionally been a few coppers cheaper than the average high street greengrocer would charge, and a weekly tour of the market stalls could save a shilling or two here and there, and stretch the inadequate housekeeping money a little bit further. Mill Lane was just one of the fruit market's various homes over the years. The date of this photograph is January 1953 - a nippy season for traders who had to attend their stall, stamping their feet against the biting winds of winter, and no doubt they were glad to pop into the nearby snack bar for a warming mug of tea from time to time. Interestingly, the garlands and baubles hanging in some of the windows in the background remind us that Christmas had only recently been celebrated when this view was captured.

Below: 'Closing down!' shouts the huge sign that is prominently displayed high on the frontage of UKAY Discount Furnishing Centre, and the added words give the reason for the closure as expiration of lease. It was a dry day when the scene was caught on camera in July 1977, which was fortunate as it allowed UKAY to display their range of furniture to tempt passers by to update their sitting room or dining room with a new three-piece suite or table and chairs. What a pity that we can't read and marvel at the bargain prices!

We must hope for their sake that the rain held off and that their advertising campaign, which told us that 'all stock must be cleared' (using the side of Raebur House as a convenient advertising hoarding), paid off.

More than a few Cardiff couples will be able to remember putting a little cash aside each week towards furniture for their very first home. By the time they tied the knot the happy couple would have enough in the kitty to buy furniture - and for many that would mean browsing happily around the UKAY showroom in Frederick Street, where the choice was wide and the prices were just right.

Bottom: Do you remember collecting Green Shield Stamps? The little green stamps were highly popular during the 1960s and 70s, and were given to customers on a range of different goods by hundreds of stores and garages. Week by week we stuck them carefully in their little books until we had a nice little stack of them. Then came the red letter day, when we had filled enough books to take along and exchange them for gifts, which could be anything from a handbag to a set of kitchen scales or mixing bowls. Exactly when Green Shield Stamps disappeared from the scene is not recalled, but today we can buy the latest CD or video from the same spot. In the premises adjoining the Green Shield Stamp shop in this 1979 view, P&O Travel have set up shop, helping Cardiffians to choose their next relaxing holiday 'away from it all'. Further along the new block, however, apart from the Co-op Bank the units are empty and in fact appear to be still unfinished. It took us some time to adjust to these typical 1970s 'square block' buildings, which never seemed to take on the character of the familiar Victorian buildings that many of us had grown up with.

At work

Left: The stately tower of St John the Baptist watches serenely over this scene of frantic activity, where vans and cars squeeze past each other and shoppers laden with baskets and bags take their lives in their hands to cross Church Street. The photograph dates from December 1972, so Christmas presents of one kind and another perhaps formed part of the content of those bags!

Hemlines, notorious for rarely staying the same for more than two or three years, had reached knee length by the early 70s. The ladies caught on camera here had chosen to wear skirts, but jeans and trousers had become popular by that time with both women and men, and the window of 'Just Pants' on the right has a fine display of the 'unisex' workwear that had become high fashion.

By the 1960s denim jeans were recognised as the fashion of the decade, and they were to remain popular right up to the end of the 1990s. Denim jeans were first introduced in the 19th century, when a factory in Nimes in France produced them as heavy duty workwear. By 1998, however, younger people were beginning to turn away from denim, especially as their elders (not to mention a number of prominent political figures!) were still wearing their jeans. Far be it from the average teenager to be seen in public wearing

clothes that in any way resembled their parents' - and jeans began to lose their popularity.

Above: Within the space of a few short months this early 1950s view of The Friary was to change for ever. In the background readers will see that The Prudential building was in the process of construction, the massive structure rising floor by floor as if built with a giant meccano set. The building was completed by April 1952. In these days of rapid change, however, few things stay the same for many years, and this view was set to change again by the end of the 1990s. A further two floors were later added and it is as the Cardiff Hilton Hotel that the building steps into the new millennium. The site on the left of the photograph is still in the early stages of demolition and construction, and the building work does not appear to have affected the trade of the ladies and gents outfitters on the far left.

Years ago, the canal ran along this part of Queen Street, hence its old and more picturesque name, Crockherbtown Lock. A number of interesting vehicles can be seen here; a 'new' Morris 8 of the 1940s and a little Austin pass each other in the foreground, while following the Austin is a Sunbeam Talbot.

Quality potatoes, fine Welsh wines - and a lorry to put them in!

Cardiff's first dock, West Bute Dock, was opened in 1839, and the immense, imposing five-storey stone warehouse belonging to Edward England Limited which still stands at the top end of it today was built not long afterwards. The firm which we know as Edward England was set up in 1842 by John Humphrey England with the express purpose of supplying potatoes to Cardiff's rapidly increasing population. Mr England came to Cardiff in 1842, at the age of 25, and took premises in St Mary Street, where he stayed until he acquired the prime site at the head of West Bute Dock and had his warehouse built there. The number of potatoes that must have passed through that warehouse in the next 150 years defies the imagination; however, it may be of assistance to anybody wishing to perform this calculation to know that in 1897 1,000 tons of new potatoes were imported and distributed within the space of three days, while in 1913 volumes reached 16,000 tons a month.

John Humphrey England moved to Cardiff from Wiltshire, although he was actually born in Islington, North London, in 1817. The young man was one of many pioneers who were drawn to Cardiff, a city whose future prosperity was assured by its lucrative coalfields and its new port. The growing mining industry in South Wales was attracting large numbers of mineworkers, some from the Welsh villages but many from further afield. The workforce, once settled, would grow into a whole new community with diverse needs, and markets of all kinds would open up in the area. Between 1831 and 1907 Cardiff's population was to multiply, from 6,000 to 100,000 - around half the total population

of Wales. By 1907 Cardiff would be sufficiently important to receive a visit from King Edward VII, to open the new Queen Alexandra Dock. The people who mined the 'black diamonds' and manned what was to become the biggest port in the British Empire, exporting over 2,000,000 tons of coal in 1907, were here to stay, and they and their families needed to eat, so it was fortunate that John Humphrey England stepped in to make sure that they were never short of one staple food - potatoes.

Nobody, in the 19th century, ever thought of growing potatoes in England; all potatoes were imported. J H England began by shipping potatoes from Northern Ireland in small sailing vessels, and later from the Continent, in rather larger sailing vessels and steamers. The boats were unloaded by hand; a newspaper article published some years later, in 1902, refers admiringly to the 'stout lasses' who worked alongside the men in handling the cargo. There was a steam-powered conveyor belt to carry the potatoes from the quayside to the warehouse, and from there they were destined to go by horse and cart, either directly to their destination or to the railway station. The business was soon well-established, and, having settled happily in Cardiff, the successful young entrepreneur married Anne Rees of Pembroke, whose father had rendered invaluable assistance against the French invasion of 1797. The story goes that he helped mobilise all the women of Fishguard with coracles, which are five-foot-long canvas boats, and led them round and round the point to frighten the French; somehow this ruse worked, and the French fled. John and Anne had a

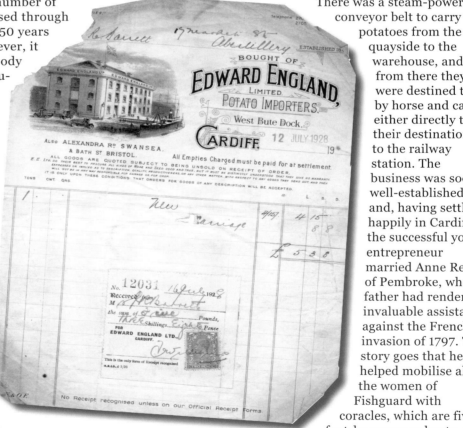

Above: An early letterhead. **Top:** *John Humphrey England, founder of the company.*

large family and two of their sons, Edward and Richard, in due course joined their father's firm; the potato business continued to grow, and by the time of John's death on 27th August 1887, at the age of 69, there was a thriving concern to be handed down to the second generation.

Edward, who lived at Eastbrook Hall, Dinas Powis and later at Y Parc with his wife Louise Lewis, continued to build up the potato trade at West Dock; his brother Richard who lived at Rumney Court was also involved for a time, but began business on his own account in 1876. They used the same sources of supply as their father had, but also began importing from Holland and Poland and in particular from Brittany. Their markets expanded to cover South Wales and into the Midlands; their first branch office was opened in Swansea in 1904, followed by an office in Bristol in 1905, and in that year too the firm became a Limited Company with Edward England, Mr J H Mullins of

Above: The premises in the early days. Below: The port of Cardiff at the turn of the 20th century.

Llandaff and Mr T F North of Radyr, who was to remain with the company until 1945, as directors. Edward's son Jack joined the company the following year; Richard's son had had a brief career there but, like his father, had left in 1895 to set up independently, trading as a potato merchant in Cardiff from 1895.

As the busiest port in Britain, Cardiff was enjoying great prosperity. By 1907 the overall tonnage exported from Cardiff to countries overseas was greater than that of any other port in Great Britain, and therefore greater than any other port in the world; Cardiff was the second most important port in the British Isles for the import of timber and iron ore, and the principal port for the import of potatoes. In the early potato season there was great competition amongst the local potato merchants to be the first to get their consignments of new potatoes from Brittany, and as the speed of the ship was obviously a critical factor, Edward England commissioned shipbuilders Fullerton of Glasgow to build a small, fast steamer for the company in 1909. SS Cardiff City, as the 322 ton

vessel was christened, cost £6,200 and proved ideal for the small ports of Britanny and Northern Ireland, and took an average of just five days to travel from Cardiff to Treguier in Britanny and back.

Having speeded up the sea crossing, the company then set about cutting down the time taken to deliver the potatoes to their final destination. By this time motor transport had become an option; again, mathematically-minded readers might like to compare £279-1s-6d which the company spent on horses and carts in 1905, and the £185-16s-6d which it spent on stabling in 1911, with the cost of a Leyland truck in 1924: £585.0s.0d. However, the company purchased its first motor lorry in 1913 and clearly considered it a good investment, as horses began to be phased out from then on. So by 1914 some 33 shiploads of potatoes were arriving each month, the company had its own ship and its own lorries, and prospects must have seemed excellent. Then war broke out. Jack England was commissioned as a gunner and spent the war in the trenches in Northern France, taking part in both battles of the Somme; miraculously, he survived. SS Cardiff City was attacked by a German U-boat off the coast of Ireland but managed to get away, and continued travelling the seas until she was shipwrecked in 1930. Sadly, Edward England did not live to see the end of the war; he died in 1917, and Major Jack England took over the management of the company when he returned from active service.

Above: *Major Jack England at the Somme, 1916.*
Top: *An early aerial view of the premises.*

The company continued to thrive. The firm of Messrs J O Nash of Plymouth was purchased in 1920, followed by Robert Nicholson's potato export business at Kilkeel, Co. Down; these potatoes had the registered trade mark of Shamrock Brand Greencastle Potatoes. There were plans to make Ireland a still more important source of supply later in the decade when the spread of the Colorado Beetle in Northern France led to a ban on the import of French potatoes; the company opened a branch in Galway in 1928 and began to encourage the Galway farmers to grow early seed potatoes for planting on the coast of Southern Ireland. However, economic difficulties arose; but meanwhile Jack, who liked to spend his summer holidays in St Davids, had realised that parts of Pembrokeshire had a mild enough climate to grow potatoes. Jack England entered into negotiation with the Potato Board and ICI, local farmers were persuaded to experiment in growing early potatoes, and by 1935 a successful scheme was being operated, with Edward England providing the seed, the fertiliser and a guarantee to market the entire crop of the 190 farmers who had registered with the Pembrokeshire Marketing Scheme. The growers received payment which was calculated on the average price of Jersey potatoes that week. The scheme was successful; by 1943 200 tons of Pembrokeshire potatoes were marketed, and by 1946 423 farmers were taking part. The Pembrokeshire new potato, launched through the efforts of Edward England Limited, has brought us many popular varieties over the years, with memorable names like Great Scott, Golden Wonder, Edzell Blue, British Queen, Arran Comrade and, intriguingly, What's Wanted.

> *In the early 1950s Robert Norris began to introduce new ideas to the business*

The second world war again took its toll on the family; Major Jack England was once again called to arms and spent many nights manning the anti-aircraft batteries protecting Cardiff's docks; Captain Robert Norris, his future son-in-law, was severely wounded in 1942, and Wing Commander Richard Geoffrey England was tragically shot down over Holland on one of the last sorties of the war, aged 27.

In January 1954 - around the time that shipping stopped using the West Dock, bringing a great era to an end - Jack England's middle daughter Rosalind married Captain R V Norris, who left his previous post with the Reed Paper Group in Kent to become managing director of his new father-in-law's company. Robert Norris brought new ideas to the business; he expanded into fruit, purchasing a fruit farm at East Farleigh, near

Below left: *Rosalind England, who married Robert Norris. Rosalind is still very active in the business today.* **Below:** *Captain Robert Norris.*

Maidstone, Kent, in 1960 and went on to become one of the founder members of the Cardiff Wholesale Fruit Centre, better known as the Market, which was formed at about the same time that the West Dock was filled in, in the mid 1960s. For the first time, fresh fruit from Kent was available daily in Cardiff, courtesy of Edward England; lorries would be loaded up in Kent in the evening and would travel to Cardiff overnight, and in the morning fresh strawberries and cherries could be purchased at Cardiff Market by those who arrived before stocks ran out. Whilst these days we rather take it for granted that we should be able to buy whatever we want where and when we want it, this was nonetheless quite a feat in the early 1960s, when long-distance road transport was a relatively new concept. Edward England already had its own fleet of lorries, and the journey from Kent to Cardiff was scheduled with a change of driver in the middle of the night.

Robert's son Richard joined the business in 1971 and took over three years later when his father died suddenly. His brother Robert joined him in 1975, and two years later they bought a potato farm in Herefordshire, which at its peak was growing over 100-acres of potatoes a year.

An exciting new venture launched by Richard and Robert in the 1980s was the planting of a six-acre vineyard on the outskirts of Cowbridge. Red, white and rose wine is produced and marketed under the label Glyndwr - the label itself depicts the Prince Owain Glyndwr in front of his stronghold Castell

Carreg Cennen. Both reds and whites have already won various awards from the wine industry; the range includes a Burgundy-style red and a sparkling white. Although the Welsh climate does not guarantee exceptional sunshine, it does have the advantage of long daylight hours, and this is one of the reasons for the high quality of Welsh wines. It is believed that the Romans planted a large vineyard at Caerleon, near Newport; archae-ologists have discovered ruins, and fossilised grape pips, on the site. Today there are a dozen or so vineyards in South Wales. Production at Glyndwr

Top: The premises in the 1980s.
Above: The family today with their local MP. From left to right: Robert Norris, Walter Sweeney MP, Richard Norris, Rosalind Norris at the launch of their sparkling wine.

currently runs at around 20,000 bottles a year, from a total of 6,000 vines, which makes it one of Wales' largest vineyards.

A rather more prosaic but, again, extremely successful diversification came about when the company established a garage on Collingdon Road which was initially an extension of the firm's road haulage operations, but which began to provide mechanical and bodywork repair services for commercial vehicles belonging to other companies and build commercial vehicle bodies as well as maintaining the England fleet. This venture has grown rapidly; now a subsidiary company in its own right, England's Truck Care moved to its current site on Hadfield Road when it outgrew the Collingdon Road site; in 1994 it became the main Renault truck dealership in South Wales and currently supplies vehicles to a number of local firms.

A greengrocery in the old market town of Cowbridge is the third and smallest of the firm's new ventures in recent years, but one which deserves a mention because it is so very much appreciated by the locals who shop there.

However, these interesting diversifications have in no way diminished England's interest in potatoes. Trade at the warehouse is as brisk this century as it was last, albeit with artics to load and unload instead of the perhaps more picturesque sailing ships. The staff, as one would expect from a fifth-generation family concern, includes many long-serving employees, some with 30 years' service or more, and the company prides itself on its team spirit. Many retired members of staff call in for a chat and a cup of coffee with their former colleagues, and a lot of happy memories are preserved in the stories that people never tire of hearing. Customers include many catering outlets, especially the fish and chip trade, which can also obtain cooking fats and other goods from Edward England. Seed potatoes are supplied to farmers and garden centres, and there is a strong seasonal trade in Christmas trees. But whatever they buy, Edward England's customers enjoy a very personal service from the company which is synonymous with the supply of quality potatoes throughout South Wales all year round. Edward England has been doing this for more than one and a half centuries, and has no intention of stopping!

Left: *The company's shop in Cowbridge.*
Below: *Directors and staff, celebrating 150 years in business - 1992.*

Shipping ahead with Graig, steady as a Rock

Ginger haired Idwal Williams, a coal trimmer's son, worked his way to fame and fortune by attending evening book keeping classes. On qualifying (as a Pupil Teacher!) he worked for a short time in the Glamorgan Education Office before joining the Bristol Steam Navigation Company as a book-keeper. His next step up the ladder was as Assistant Accountant with Furness Withy where he introduced Double Entry book keeping and multiple carbon pads before the Great War. Childhood injuries prevented his enlistment so he spent 1914-1918 doing the work of five men aided by one fifth of the peacetime typing complement.

In 1919 five different groups considered that the thirty five year old Idwal Williams was the ideal person to manage the new Graig Shipping Company to be run by Idwal Williams & Co. He left Furness Withy taking Colum Tudball, an office boy who rose to Managing Director, as staff. The company's first ship was a 5,000 ton steamer, the SS 'War Down', equipped with both electric light and Mr Marconi's 'Wireless'. She cost £140,000 and was renamed SS 'Graig' (Welsh for rock), under Captain T C Smith, Master. She was then chartered for two years to carry South African coal from Durban to Kilindini in Kenya, after which profitable enterprise she was sold for £30,000.

At the time steam ships ran on Welsh coal and there followed a brief flirtation with the ownership of a coalmine which was eventually sold to the adjacent colliery. The second SS 'Graig', a four hold general cargo vessel similar to the first, was built for the company, in 1924, in Port Glasgow for employment as a Tramp Steamer to go where cargoes were to be picked up rather than running the regular routes of a 'liner'. She was joined in 1932 by M D J Hooper, a fourteen year old cabin boy, or junior steward, who retired as the firm's Commodore (Senior Captain) in 1982. Those were the days when advancement went to experience, and qualifications (ie Mate's and Master's

Top left: *Idwal Williams in a picture dating from a few years before he died.*
Above centre: *The first balance sheet of the company, showing the SS Graig at her purchase price of £140, 000.*
Below: *The first Master and Officers of the SS Graig.*

Like other ambitious seamen M D J Hooper worked his way from the fo'c's'l, the Merchant Marine equivalent of the 'lower deck' of the RN, by guts and hard work. Twenty years after joining Graig as cabin boy he took command, think of what that expression means, in 1952, as Master Mariner (Captain) of his first Graig ship.

The Graig Shipping Company adopted the custom of naming all its ships with the prefix 'Graig' so that all its ships were in logical sequence in Lloyd's Register from Graigaur, Gold Rock, to Graigwerdd, Green Rock. The 'house flag' is a true reflection of the Welsh flag, white over green, superimposed by a large red 'G', instead of a red dragon, as displayed on all the Company's vessels.

tickets), won on the job rather than to the inexperienced qualified college leaver.

This youngster bought a Donkey's Breakfast (a straw palliase) for half a crown (12.5p) to go under bedding supplied from home before voyaging, laden with Welsh coal, for inland ports up the River Plate, between Brazil and the Argentine. In spite of two accidents to the ship in her two year voyage the lad became enthralled by life at sea, regardless of the iron discipline which kept locked the tap of the limited water supply. This in the days when 'salt junk' (salted meat) and 'hard tack' (ship's biscuits), the same rations as served in Nelson's day, were normal fare supplemented by dried peas and jam, tea and tinned milk. Personal washing was allowed half a bucket of water per day!

During those twenty years the British Merchant Marine was pre-eminent as the world's major cargo carrying service. In the inter-war years no less than seventeen shipping companies operated out of Cardiff; today Graig Shipping is the lone local survivor.

The effects of the Wall Street 'Crash' of 1929 had banks closing down shipping firms at the rate of one per day during the desperate years of the Depression. Graig managed to keep up the payments on the company's two ships. This difficult task was assisted by the installation in 1933, at a cost of £6,000 per vessel, of the new North East

Top: The SS Graig while on her two year charter.
Above: The launching party for the MV Glynafon. Idwal Williams is on the far left. Desmond Williams is in the centre.

Marine Superheat machinery, which recycled steam at a saving of one eighth of the total daily coal consumption. Unable to obtain a loan from the bank Idwal Williams, thanks to a generous referee, persuaded the manufacturers to allow him to pay by installments, completed in nine months. In the same year he took on the profitable agency to sell North Eastern Marine machinery throughout Southern England which lasted until they were taken over in 1980.

Graig survived the dividend-less early years of the 1930s ready to enter the war in which submarine warfare, air attacks and surface raiders devastated the British Merchant Marine. Graig managed several new ships for the Ministry of Defence during the second world war and bought them when sold off on the cessation of hostilities. In November 1945 Idwal Williams strengthened the board by appointing John, George Williams' son, and Idwal's sons Dillwyn and Desmond Williams, partners in Idwal Williams & Company and directors of The Graig Shipping Company Ltd. The latter partner was still serving in the forces of the Crown and returned to 'civvy street' in July 1946.

Having survived the bombs and fires which had plagued Cardiff during hostilities the company's records were destroyed in a fire which wrecked Merthyr House in the first year of peace. Desmond learned the ship-broking business from Colum Tudball, the former office boy now a director, and, in 1948, was sent to Canada to learn the rudiments of

Top: *SS Graigaur loading trucks and munitions in London Docks at the start of the Suez Crisis.*
Above right: *MV Graiglas.*

life at sea. Following a change in business liability Desmond went to the Baltic Exchange in London for a year prior to opening the firm's London office in 1951, from which he arranged a 'round the world voyage' in SS 'Graigaur' for his parents. During that journey a temporary Assistant Steward, working his passage home from Australia for a shilling (5p) a day, did a painting of the ship which still hangs in the company offices. Unfortunately modern regulations prevent such enterprise by young travellers.

The 1952 purchase of the Basra Shipping Company introduced diesel powered engines to Graig. Next year Desmond's honeymoon was interrupted when he went to the Outer Hebrides to supervise the salvage of SS 'Graigaur' on charter to the Russians, an operation aided by a muscular Dutch woman and a hospitable Post Mistress! The repaired vessel was later requisitioned, in 1956, to carry munitions of war for the Suez landing. By this time Graig were operating diesel powered Motor Vessels such as the MV 'Glynafon', and the MV 'Graigfelen' formerly under Swiss ownership. The SS 'Graigaur' was sold to a Greek; as he failed on the payments the ship was arrested by radio and sold to the Chinese after the crew had been flown home to Greece.

The decline in freight rates caused Graig to lay up in 1962, in the River Fal, all three of its ships. A year later the MV 'Graig' was sold to a Hong Kong company. The introduction of government Shipbuilding Loans to help both British ship building and shipping companies stay afloat was seized upon by Graig as the opportunity to acquire more realistically sized craft than the 9,000 ton unladen dead weight ships of the past. Although looking at 15,000, and even 18,000, tons dw Graig were persuaded to invest in a 28,300 ton dw bulk-carrier named 'Graigwerdd'. This proved so profitable to operate that the two small Motor Vessels were immediately sold.

An even more revolutionary government policy gave Investment Grants on ships built anywhere in the world. Graig bought the Japanese built MV 'East Breeze', renamed 'Glyntaf', which had furniture made for the smaller oriental crew. The hard working Chinese crew was retained under British officers who adapted happily to the racial differences in which not only were the Chinamen more thrifty caterers but the wives of the leave bound crew cleaned ship prior to inspection by the wives of the relief crew! Although the late 60s and early 70s saw ship owners enjoying a strong freight market Graig realised that things were changing. The Polish built SS 'Glyntawe', a bulk cargo carrier with all accommodation and engines aft, was chartered to the old Italian company of Grimaldi Brothers at the same time as MV 'Glyntaf' was sold to help pay for her.

Below: *MV Graiglas never traded for the company.*

Memories of CARDIFF

In 1971, when Idwal Williams died, Desmond became chairman and Colum Tudball was appointed as MD. A consortium of Canadian oil interests approached Graig which led to the company becoming involved, with Syd Kahanoff's Voyager Petroleum Co, in on shore oil exploration in Southern England. Another new venture was the short term ownership of Reigate Travel Ltd, bought in 1971 for £48,000, to save travel costs on crew transfers, and sold in 1980 for £140,000. Other opportunities grasped in that decade included the rapid, and profitable, purchase and sale six months later of the MV 'Cluden'. Colum Tudball finally retired in 1973 after loyally serving Graig since 1919. The next ship ordered by Graig was the second MV 'Garthnewydd' built in Spain but sold before launching, to an Indian company, at a $1M profit. This was replaced by the much smaller Spanish built bulk carrier, Torre-del-Oro, bought from a Greek and renamed 'Graigaur' (Gold Rock). She was badly damaged by a giant wave when carrying Mauritius sugar to Canada after which the icy waters of the Great Banks stripped paint off the bridge and froze the sugar so hard that it was chipped out of the holds by pneumatic drills. Life at sea has its exciting moments.

'Nothing venture nothing gained' is a doctrine practised by Graig, always ready to try something worthwhile. One such novelty was the purchase, in revolutionary Portugal, of delicious Vintage Port sold two years later, in 1978, at a 25% per annum profit. Well, the company was founded by a qualified teacher and they're capable of anything!

The Japanese built MV 'Graigwen' and MV 'Graiglwyd' were bought equipped with twenty ton swl (safe working load) hydro-electric cranes at each hatch, which rendered the ships independent of loading and discharging facilities and shore labour problems.

Politics, like economics and war, affect the lives of sailormen and ship owners alike, sometimes to their benefit. Graig won a UN contract to ship fifty houses, intended for the UN Peace-keeping Force in the disputed Sinai Desert, from the USA to Egypt. As the house moving lorries were too wide for an Egyptian bridge UNO ordered the ships to off-load in Israel. Graig pointed out the loss of trade which would arise from a likely Arab embargo on a shipping company seen trading with the tough successful Israelis. To everyone's pleasant surprise the whole business was resolved without costly black-listing or even 'baksheesh'.

These days it takes around a year to build a ship to the unfinished delivery stage prior to fitting out. The actual launch takes place soon after the half way stage after which the engine, having passed its dry tests, is dismantled and reconstructed inside the hull. The accommodation and bridge departments are then installed and the vessel is ready for her sea trials, rather like the road tests of a car. Remember, ships have no brakes. Some of the huge monster tankers of the 1960s needed eight miles or more to come to a stop!

Below: *Graigfelen transiting one of the locks in the St Lawrence Seaway.*

Britain, despite the loaded dice of subsidised foreign competition. The Company has now gone into a joint venture with Clipper Denmark to build ten 9,000 tons deadweight multi-purpose project vessels having two 150 ton heavy lift cranes, a capacity to load 640 containers - 106 of which can be refrigerated and having a speed of 16.5 knots.

As this is the 80th anniversary of the Company, Cardiff, and Wales, can be proud of the achievements of this truly Welsh shipping company as she sails confidently into the Twenty First Century.

Above and left: *Graigwerdd, built in 1964 was launched by Anne Williams.*
Below: *m/v 'Clipper Cardiff photographed on her maiden voyage from Kobe to Rotterdam with amongst other cargo, a 1200 tonne main engine for one of the largest container ships ever built.*

The British shipping industry, which 'saved our bacon' in two world wars and enabled us to retain the Falkland Islands, pays its way with no help from government sources.

Other countries subsidise their land, air and sea freight and passenger carrying services because they recognise the value of these as profitable businesses. Graig is proud to be part of an industry which earns considerable foreign currency for

The successful company that doesn't waste energy on hot air

Hot air, cold air, clean air, dehumidified air - MacWhirter is today one of the pioneers of environmental engineering, with energy conservation always one of its top priorities. In fact, the company has been finding ways of using energy to good effect for well over a century. One of the very first devices patented under the McWhirter name was a voltmeter and ammeter for measuring electricity, invented in 1883 by the company's founder, William McWhirter (1851-1933).

William McWhirter was born in Ayr in 1851, studied at Newton-on-Ayr Academy, and began a career in telegraphy and railway work, employed by the Post Office telegraph department and then by a number of other firms before becoming telegraph engineer for Furness Railways in 1876. In 1880, while still working for Furness Railways, he also became partner in an electrical engineering venture, Norman & Son, and he launched a branch of this firm in Glasgow in 1882; this was the business which was to evolve into the firm of MacWhirter Limited. The following year William McWhirter (1851-1933)

Left: *Mr Anthony MacWhirter (1876-1949).*
Below and bottom: *Penarth Road Electrical Workshop 1912.*

left his job as telegraph engineer to concentrate on lighting contracts, and he also patented his invention of a combined volmeter and ammeter for measuring and indicating both ac and dc electrical currents in a circuit, which he registered as a 'new or improved electric meter' in July 1883. After various improvements and refinements to the original design, he eventually handed its manufacture over to the General Electric Company, and it became the basis for virtually every electricity meter in common use.

Meanwhile, the Glasgow branch of Norman & Son became McWhirter & Sons and moved to Govan. William McWhirter (1851-1933) married Marian, a girl from his home town of Ayr. His eldest son, Anthony (born in Barrow on 13th June 1876), who grew up sharing his father's interest in all things electrical, studied at the Glasgow & West of Scotland Technical College while working for his father.

In 1900 Anthony went to America to work for GEC Electrical Company of New York, gaining useful experience and finally becoming one of their trouble shooters, which took him all over the USA. While over there, to help the Americans pronounce his name, he had it altered to MacWhirter by deed poll and they were then sure he was Scottish and not Irish. Ironically though, Anthony's future lay neither in America nor his native Scotland. He returned - as Anthony MacWhirter - to Glasgow in 1905, supposedly on leave, but while he was there he married Jessie and decided not to go back to America. When he rejoined his father's company, however, his reputation as a troubleshooter followed him back home and he was in great demand all over

Above: Electrical Workshops delivery lorry 1920.
Top: Works outing 1937.

tions nationwide. The firm's first female employee, a 17 year old, in her later years described the Wharf Street offices as a cheerless, one-storey building divided into two rooms where office hours were from 9am to 5.30pm Monday to Friday and 9am to 1pm on Saturdays. Of Mr MacWhirter himself she wrote, "He was a worker". She recalled that he was constantly on the go, away to London, Nottingham, Swansea, Glasgow etc., all in the course of business. She also remembered him as something of a 'dour Scot', and indeed after working there for three years, she left to take a job at the Gaumont Film Company, where she

the country. One job for which his services were sought was a contract for special repairs work in South Wales, including work on the power station at Roath, Cardiff, and there proved to be sufficient work there to occupy him on a permanent basis. So Anthony settled in Cardiff in 1912 and this city thereafter became the headquarters of the firm's opera-

Top: Mr Anthony MacWhirter and his three daughters shortly after World War I. **Above:** *Refrigeration department service vans in the 1930s.*

received a salary of £1 a week, a 33% increase on MacWhirter's 15/- a week!

Dour Scot or no, Anthony MacWhirter became a very well-known figure in electrical engineering. In 1913 he became the first Chairman of the newly-formed Electrical Contractors Association in South Wales; he was also honorary treasurer of the South Wales Branch of the Association of Mining Electrical and Mechanical Engineers for 33 years, and acted as Branch President in 1925. He certainly remained a true Scot at heart, and was President of the Caledonian Society in 1947; while another of his more unusual distinctions was that of being the only male member of the Electrical Association for Women. The training of apprentices was an issue to which he attached great importance, and he was instrumental in the setting up in Cardiff of a 'day-release' scheme run jointly by the technical college and industry, enabling apprentices to attend college one day a week.

Having been involved in both electrical contracting and auto electrics until the mid 30s, in 1934 the Cardiff branch of the firm took over the local Kelvinator agency and began to specialise in refriger-ation. The heavy electrical repair side was sold in 1935, and the rest of the business moved to Penarth Road, Cardiff as MacWhirter Ltd, where a new refrig-eration department was formed, and the following year this department was awarded the Kelvinator Cup,

in recognition of its achievement in recording the highest turnover of Kelvinator businesses in the UK.

By 1938 the firm was employing a total office staff of eight - at salaries varying between £2-7s-6d and 15/- per week - and running six vans, of which three were assigned to the Kelvinator Department, two to the Exide Department and one to the General Department. Subsequent years saw a continued emphasis the sales and service of refrigeration equipment and industrial air conditioning units; customers included hotels, boarding houses, fruit merchants, grocers and dairymen, and, to a lesser extent, the domestic market. One of the most successful new products launched by the company was the Kelmac Milk Cooler, which proved very popular with local farmers, more and more of whom were beginning to use electricity. Washing machines were also becoming increasingly popular; the firm had a radio department; and one innovation which seems to have no connection whatsoever with the general activities of the firm, but which is far too intriguing to go unmentioned, is Anthony MacWhirter's invention of a trackless hare for use in greyhound racing. His first hares were installed in London, at West Ham and Wembley Stadiums. By the time the second world war broke out, the company had moved to a new site on North Road,

Below: *The showroom in St Mary Street in the 1930s when the depot was in Wharf Street.*

having outgrown its Penarth Road premises. They became the Admiralty contractors in Wales, carrying out a great deal of work for the War Office and being responsible for modifications to Asdic equipment.

Anthony MacWhirter died in 1949 at the age of 73, leaving a widow, one son and three daughters. The business passed to his son, called, after the family tradition, William. Expansion continued steadily after the war. In 1971 new buildings were added to the North Road premises, and a branch was opened in Netham Road, Bristol, in 1979. By this time William's son Anthony had this time joined the business. In 1982 the company celebrated its 100th anniversary with a special luncheon in Cardiff Castle, at which one of the guests was Mr William MacWhirter's cousin Norris McWhirter CBE, editor of the Guinness Book of Records.

The company has adapted itself over the years to the changing needs of the commercial and industrial environment

Above: *The North Road premises in 1982.*

The main focus of the company's work has shifted over the years, adapting itself in increasingly sophisticated ways to the needs of the industrial and commercial environment. It was during the 1970s that it first established itself as a supplier of air conditioning for computer firms - including clients in Scotland - and began exporting package air conditioning to all parts of the world. This in turn has involved the firm in international servicing contracts, for example in Yugoslavia; while closer to home MacWhirter was responsible for the installation of one of the earliest heat recovery systems at a swimming pool in South West Wales, aimed at reducing the escalating energy costs associated with operating public baths. The company was one of the early leaders in environmental engineering, designing its own specialised range of environmental control systems and pioneering the use of the heat pump. The heat pump works by absorbing unused energy from various sources and converting it into energy which can then be used for heating or cooling. Heat pumps soon became an essential part of the energy-conscious heating systems, both for domestic use and for shops, offices, supermarkets and factories. The heat pumps also continue to be used in the recuperation of waste heat from recreation and leisure facilities, which tend to be high energy users; swimming pools can effect tremendous savings by using heat pump dehumidifiers to recover the latent heat from the air and re-use it to heat the hall, the pool water and the changing rooms as well.

In July 1999, Ross MacWhirter joined the company as a school leaver to start an apprenticeship. Ross, who is the eldest son of Anthony MacWhirter, was named after Norris McWhirter's identical twin brother (and founding editor of The Guinness Book of Records),

Ross McWhirter, who was shot in his own house in November 1975 in a revenge attack by the IRA.

Today MacWhirters employs the most up-to-date techniques in providing multi-discipline services to the building industry. A whole range of services - heating, air conditioning, clean rooms, cold rooms, lighting, power, communications, waste and effluent services - can be adapted to an equally wide range of environments - residential accommodation for the elderly, hospitals, factories, offices, local authority buildings, hotels and leisure complexes. The company's in-house expertise and comprehensive facilities allow them to handle design/construct projects from planning to completion. Managed maintenance programmes ensure that all plant is kept in top working condition to maximise cost-effectiveness, efficiency and reliability. Energy conservation will continue to be a priority as we move into the 21st century - and MacWhirter, a company which is 117 years old at the time of writing, will continue to lead the way forward.

Left: *Cardiff Castle on 10th September 1982 at which the company's main guest was Mr William MacWhirter's cousin, Mr Norris McWhirter CBE, founder editor of the Guinness Book of Records (1954-1986). He is seen here holding the 1883 voltmeter and ammeter patent, flanked by Mr William MacWhirter and Anthony MacWhirter.*
Below: *In 1982, the company celebrated its 100th anniversary with a special luncheon in the Baronial Hall, Cardiff Castle.*

The family business which enjoys success on a major scale

The Welsh are renowned for having a good ear for music, and Cardiff-born Horace Gamlin has a more accurate ear than most. Music has always been an important part of Horace's life. His father Archie was a piano tuner, and some of Horace's most vivid childhood memories from the war years are of accompanying his father to the celebrity concerts held of a Sunday at the Empire Theatre, where Archie Gamlin was duty tuner. There Horace collected autographs from famous guest artistes who appeared along with the Cardiff Philharmonic Orchestra (conducted by Herbert Ware), including celebrities such as Benno Moiseiwitsch and Eileen Joyce. Another favourite venue was Cory Hall (now sadly demolished); the BBC programme Welsh Rarebit, produced by Mair Jones, went out from here every other Thursday, and Harry Secombe, Stan Stennet and other Welsh comedians destined to become household names gained their early experience on this show. Many readers will also remember another very popular radio show which Horace Gamlin was involved with in later years. For this programme, a different factory in Wales chosen for each broadcast, and Horace used to drive all over North and South Wales taking the piano to that day's location; Bert Weedon played guitar; the programme was, of course, Workers' Playtime.

Fourteen-year old Horace followed in his father's footsteps straight from school, taking an apprenticeship as a piano tuner at Dale Forty & Company, a well-known piano retailer in Cardiff. He remained here for nine years, after which he was to work for two other local retailers before setting up in business on his own: firstly for R J Heath, and subsequently for Victor Freed. While he was employed here he met his future wife Maureen, who was at that time working as a salesperson at David Morgans. After their marriage Horace set up as a piano tuner/technician, working from his own workshop. Local musicians made good use of his wealth of experience and fine skills, and by 1960 the business was sufficiently well-established for Horace and Maureen to open their own retail music shop. After much searching, they settled on premises at 248 City Road. Extensive alterations and redecoration were carried out, and by September 1960 they were ready to open their doors to customers. Pianos were - as they still are - the basis of the business; but as pop music grew into a culture in its own right and began to exert a whole range of strong new musical influences on the young, Horace was quick to respond to their needs, and he stocked the electric guitars, Vox amplifiers, sheet music and other accessories which every budding pop star needed. Gamlins was in fact the first shop in Wales to stock Fender guitars and supply the kind of amplifiers which the Shadows and the Beatles were using. Horace and Maureen's shop became a popular rendezvous spot for the members of local groups, and amongst the regulars who spent many an hour there was a certain Tommy Scott, the singer with The Senators; Tommy Scott, of course, is better known today as Tom Jones.

Backed by Horace's technical knowledge and expertise and Maureen's sales experience, the business went from strength to strength. Some two years after opening their shop in City

Below: *A float in the Lord Mayor's Parade passing the shop.*

Road, they decided to separate the two sides of the business, moving the pianos and organs into an exclusive showroom in a building just opposite their original premises, in Richmond Road. Then, before the expiration of the lease at City Road, an existing music business in Wyndam Arcade became available following a bereavement. Gamlins bought it, and this became their main outlet. Before long the Wyndam Arcade shop became so busy that they realised they would have to expand into larger premises. In October 1967 they moved to St Mary Street, where initially they occupied the ground floor of number 55. Two years later they were able to acquire the first floor of the same building, formerly the home of the City Conservative Club. This meant that they could separate the two sides the business again; a lift was installed, and the first floor became the piano and organ showroom, with the other instruments and accoutrements downstairs. This arrangement worked very well; the business developed in all directions, catering for every musical taste from the classical, through the popular, to the progressive, experimental and more offbeat, and offering a full range of traditional instruments while keeping up to date with the latest innovative developments in the electronic field. Then, just as the 14-year lease on 55 St Mary Street was nearing its end, an opportunity arose to acquire the larger freehold property next door, at number 56. This was ideal, providing as it did a much larger area on three floors, with a depth of 170 feet from front to back. Gamlins secured the building and transferred the business there in 1980, after carrying out major structural alterations which included having a central heating system put in, installing a lift to all three floors, and redecorating.

This has remained Gamlins' home ever since. When St Marys Street was designated an area for regeneration for the new millennium, Gamlins had the exterior of the building restored to its early 20th century glory. The restoration work, which included completely rebuilding the front wall and parapet using modern materials to recreate its historical and traditional architectural character, was nominated for a Design Award in 1974 under the Lord Mayor's Civic Awards Scheme. Inside this splendid building, Horace and Maureen have used the space to create a departmental music store, with trained staff on hand in each department to offer specialist advice and technical assistance. In the basement is the Drum Dive, a paradise for percusssionists. At the front of the store on the ground floor is the printed music - very much the domain of Mrs Gamlin - and next to that are the brass and woodwind instruments, a display of guitars and basses second to none, and amplifiers and PA equipment. For customers requiring guitar set-ups and repairs, Gamlins offers the services of Mr Rob Crocker, a talented guitar-maker and technician who works on the premises. Brass and woodwind are also serviced in store.

Above: *A drum display.* **Top:** *The first floor piano showroom.*

A wide selection of keyboards and electronic pianos can be found at the rear of the ground floor, while upstairs on the first floor is the large piano showroom which, with its stock of many grands and uprights including a selection of second-hand pianos, covers every price bracket, and offers customers a choice of shape and colour with pianos designed to enhance the decor of any home. A complete delivery service is provided; and for parents who are hesitating to invest in a piano for their child in case its enthusiasm for learning to play proves short-lived, a rental option is available. As Horace no longer has time to tune all the pianos himself, the piano department employs a piano tuner and technician, and has its own workshop which provides comprehensive repair and overhaul facilities. Gamlins also operates a professional concert hire service.

Also on the first floor is Gamlins Technic Music Academy, which organises local, area and national competitions and offers successful contestants the opportunity to perform at concerts organised world-wide by Technic - in Japan, Canada, Germany and elsewhere. Gamlins also has a longstanding connection with the Associated Board of the Royal Schools of Music, and is one of the Board's largest examining centres outside London. Examinations are staged by the Board three times a year, and Gamlins is responsible for examining more than 3,000 candidates annually. Two studios are used for the exams; each of the three examination sessions lasts for a six week period, and during that time candidates of all ages, from the very junior to the very senior, come along to take graded theoretical and practical examinations on an extremely wide variety of instruments - while the staff, ever helpful, keep a watchful eye out, ready to render assistance to small or frail candidates bearing large instruments such as harps and double basses!

Since Horace and Maureen started their business there have been many developments and changes in musical instruments. Electric organs arrived on the scene, enjoyed great popularity for a time, and were then largely superseded by modern electronic keyboards which can produce a truly amazing range of synthesised effects. There is still a limited demand for electronic organs, often for use in churches, but the one-man band is now a familiar phenomenon with keyboards providing music in bars, schools and homes everywhere. Similarly the digital piano, first launched around a decade ago, has had a significant impact upon the sales of the conventional piano; it is portable, requires no tuning, and can be used with headphones - advantages which make it particularly attractive to travelling musicians or those with little opportunity to practise out of earshot of

Above: *Part of the classic guitar display.*
Top: *The company's van and awning at a fete.*

their neighbours. One would have thought that it would be difficult to take the piano further in its development but not so! Who would have thought it possible to plug a pair of headphones into a piano, even a grand piano, so as to play without disturbing others? Such a piano exists - it is called the silent piano. The hammer action can be disengaged by pressing a pedal while the digital piano is incorporated into the key action giving you the feel of a real piano, with the benefit of digital technology. And what about one stage further? You may recall the pianola - a very large and cumbersome piano with a maze of pipes and tubes inside - that played itself (pneumatically) with the aid of pre-recorded paper rolls. Today's version is better and more versatile. A floppy disc replaces the roll, giving you a wealth of pre-recorded material and if that's not enough, you are also able to record your own playing. The Yamaha Disklavier will record all of the key and pedal movements and play back to you exactly as you played them. You can also save this information onto a floppy disc and with the addition of a sound module to the equation you can be provided with an orchestral backing to a solo piano with selected pre-recorded software.

However, for most people there can be no substitute for the traditional piano; many find pleasure in playing or listening to a favourite melody on a Yamaha grand, while for others the instrument's appeal lies in its versatility and its ability to create unforgettable sounds in styles ranging from classical to contemporary, ragtime, jazz, blues, rock 'n' roll or pop. Horace himself still sees the piano as being very much the core of the business.

Horace has made an immense contribution to the music business both locally and nationally, having been a member of the council of the Music Retailers' Association for 30 years and President for two years, bringing two successful conferences to our city, and also served as President of the

Chamber of Trade in Cardiff. He has regularly attended trade fairs in Britain, at Frankfurt and in the USA, and has travelled the world visiting manufacturers in Europe and the Far East, keeping abreast of the latest developments and arranging for pianos to be imported.

Gamlins has maintained close links with the local schools, offering a school instrument rental service for brass, woodwind, stringed instrument and percussion; and an important and eagerly-anticipated event for many Gwent schools is the prestigious Schools' Concert, held annually at St David's Hall in Cardiff, where the Gamlin Young Musician Award is presented.

A second branch of Gamlins was opened in Newport in 1980; originally situated in High Street, it subsequently moved to Commercial Street, and has been managed throughout by Mr Hugh Morgan. Like the Cardiff branch it has three floors and is organised in departments, with all the relevant services.

Plans for the future include opening the Richmond Road premises, which Gamlins still own, as a music school; at present Gamlins provides tuition at St Marys Street, where the third floor is equipped with three studios, one of which is used for guitar lessons.

In 1976 Horace and Maureen's son Philip joined the business in Cardiff. With Philip now in charge of the overall management, and grandson William and granddaughter Isobel set to follow the family tradition, Gamlins' future looks bright.

Below: *Mr and Mrs Gamlin with Mr David Owen and his wife (guest speaker) when Mr Gamlin was President of the Music Retailer Association at an Awards ceremony in the Cafe Royal, London.*

BJM for everything, immediately

The BJM approach is based on a service of stocking what the customer wants, when they want it, and providing the next day anything not in stock. Customers who are welcomed and treated like that have kept on coming since 1914 when the firm started.

FW Browning, ET Jones and J Morris were successful salesmen in secure employment with a sound firm of builders' merchants when they decided to run their own show, just two months before war broke out in the ever volatile Balkans. Some folk do make money out of wars but those in what the government decided were inessential businesses were at the tail end of the supply list and hard put to survive.

Between the wars, in spite of the Great Depression which sacrificed Welsh industry, the trio built up a sound business. They were alive to every opportunity; using new selling techniques, finding new markets and making, and keeping, regular customers.

The three bosses, aided by their families, would hold weekend meetings followed by working all hours to produce rehashed price lists ready for their employees on the Monday. This old fashioned form of leadership is still the norm for BJM, a family firm.

As local builders found business in the depressed South Wales coal field area so poor, they travelled long distances looking for work, as many do today. Those that went to London found difficulty in obtaining the supplies they needed, let alone at sensible prices. Naturally they came to Browning, Jones and Morris.

Following a lengthy debate it was agreed, in 1929, to open a London branch in charge of the proposal's chief protagonist, ET 'Ted' Jones. He set up the London yard and office on the, then new, North Circular Road as it passed through Cricklewood. This was an exciting place and period as many handsome new factories were then being established in the clean modern industries of motor tyres, vacuum cleaners, wireless sets and electrical equipment. Some of these, now part of our architectural heritage, were built by customers of BJM.

Once again a world war interrupted the lives and businesses of millions of people. Men and women were called up for war service, supplies of all kinds were rationed and those who endeavoured to keep non

Top left: FW Browning, co-founder of the company. Above centre: ET Jones, co-founder. Left: John Morris, co-founder. Below: The Cardiff premises in the 1920s.

builder the following day. Postal methods may have changed but today customers can fax their orders to BJM, in the morning, who will load the goods onto a pallet ready to be lifted by fork lift truck onto the builder's lorry in the afternoon, as always with a smile!

In the cost conscious times of the 1990s many builders' merchants either specialise or stock only the most commonly required items and show little willingness to order for clients needing something else. BJM recognise that a builder's need for something unusual, or out of stock, is as immediate as it is for the most frequently ordered items. Builders, who cannot afford time and energy to visit or ring around

essential businesses going had the devil's own job to do so. Afterwards there was a period of shortages followed by an era of great expansion and exciting new techniques. The company returned to its peacetime occupations of making tiled fireplaces, selling bathroom fittings and supplying builders with clay pipes, chimneys and other materials.

As always service was generously given with a smile as it had been in the pre-war days when builders were able to drop a pre-addressed BJM order form into the morning post knowing that it would be received well before lunch. BJM staff would put up the order and load it onto a canal boat which would deliver the goods to the

several yards in search of this or that, have come to know that they'll get it at BJM, the people who understand the trade. In order to maintain this standard of customer service BJM employ a full time expediter to obtain special purchases for all their special customers. What's more, if the item cannot be found BJM will make up, not excuses, but something to do the job. Magic!

BJM is still a family business. The present directors are grandchildren of the founders and there is already a great-grandson in the business.

Top: The loading bay at Dumballs Road in the 1920s.
Above left: The Cardiff premises in the 1950s.

Coal - the stuff of dreams

Few ports were busier than Cardiff in the 1800s. In the vast shipping trade of the time, Cardiff was highly important to the British Empire. Many businesses flocked to the port and it was at that time that Charles Evans was apprenticed to a Newport shipbroker. He specialised in exporting Welsh coals to Europe and the Baltic before starting his own business in 1880. Evans and Co exported the high quality coals required for steam ships across the Atlantic to South American and other vital 'coaling stations'. These filling stations for ships were spread throughout the shipping lanes of the world to cater for the Royal Navy and captains and owners who recognised that Welsh coal was the best for economic steaming.

His collier ships to the Baltic returned with deck cargoes of timber from the pine forests for pit props in the South Wales coalfield. By the early 1900s the firm was one of the leading coal exporters in Cardiff, Britain's major coal port, which in 1913 exported

10.5m tons of coal. The company name was later changed to Evans & Reid Coal Company Ltd in 1922. Never a leader to avoid risk Charles Evans in 1931 took on the management of four steam ships for Barclays Bank and bought them the next year to form the Nailsea Steamship Company Ltd. This venture was followed in 1936 by the formation of the Bantham Steamship Co Ltd. In those days ships of 8,000 tons were economic to run although Charles Evans replaced the old with the up to date. With the distribution of coal becoming increasingly worldwide, the company's customers ranged from the Royal Navy to the Egyptian, Portugese and South American railway companies.

During the Great War he served as an over-age Lieutenant (he was 56), rising to Lieutenant Commander, in armed yachts patrolling the

Above: *Charles Evans, who began his working life as an apprentice to a shipbroker.*

dangerous home waters of the Irish Sea and elsewhere. Following the adventures and companionship which he found so enjoyable he continued to export coal to naval and civilian coaling stations. At the outbreak of the second world war he owned a dozen ships totalling 100,000 tons. By 1943 his own fleet was reduced to one vessel, losing the majority through enemy action, although, as ship manager for the Ministry of War Transport, he commanded over a score of freighters. This fleet was engaged in the dangerous task of bringing in munitions of war (food, weapons, fuels and industrial raw materials) and exporting the manufactured goods so vital to paying our way in war as in peace.

After the war, with the demise of the coal industry the company was forced to diversify. Consequently , the ships changed from coal bearers to general cargo vessels. This proved a milestone in the evolvement of the company.

Since then the world has changed and Evans and Reid has adapted to changing circumstances by investing in other fields so successfully that The Evans and Reid Group face the Millennium with confidence.

The shipping interests of today have become centred on Brixham in Devon where the Devon Star Off Limits Shipping Co Ltd operate as ships suppliers, somewhat on the lines of a sea-going ships chandlers. Such services are a boon to large vessels which face heavy harbour dues whenever they anchor or tie up alongside a jetty. Unlike mobile grocers Devon Star provide the vast selection of naval stores (machinery, equipment and consumables) plus the victualling (food) required to keep ships at sea. Also in Brixham is Torbay and Brixham Shipping Agents Ltd which act as agents offering import/export services, leads to

cargoes and clients and all the multifarious work formerly done by the shore based 'Ships' Husbands'. Add to this they run the local pilotage services which transfer qualified pilots between ship and shore, and vice versa, for outward bound and in-coming vessels.

The popular River Dart Steam and Leisure Boat Company has diversified from the leisure market into landownership and property investment in a way that Charles Evans, always alive to change and opportunity, would have found familiar. Bilston, near Wolverhampton, is the site of Evans and Reid's aluminium foundry while the Group is also heavily involved in rubber production and distribution. At the time of writing the company owns two manufacturing plants, one at Stanley and one at Glossop, and has established a base in France from which it distributes to other European countries.

The company has a major coke distribution service which supplies England and South Wales, as well as a coal factoring division through which the firm sells a wide variety of solid fuels. These range from anthracite from Wales to general house coal. In total, 350,000 tonnes of coal pass through the company's hands every year, which proves that despite diversification into other areas, coal remains the mainstay of the business. Today's chairman and managing director, John Phillips is confident that the future is bright for the company, and insists that this success is due in no small part to the loyal staff at all levels of the business.

All this, and property investments too, is a far cry from shipping Welsh coal out of Cardiff to coaling stations around the world's oceans in the 1800s.

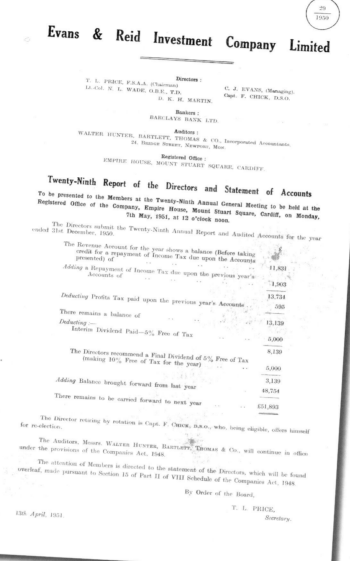

Above: The 1951 Report of Accounts which showed a profit of £51,893. Today, the Evans & Reid Group is listed in the top 200 Welsh companies.

The best education 'for Maydens for ever'

Howell's School, today part of the Girls' Day School Trust, provides girls with an opportunity to develop their talents to the full in an exciting and stimulating learning environment, acquiring the knowledge and skills to fulfil their potential while developing the moral sensitivity, independent thinking, initiative and inner resources which are the prerequisites of success and happiness in present-day society.

Society has of course changed considerably since Howell's School was first established. It was in the mid-16th century that Mr Thomas Howell, the son of a Welshman, who had made his fortune through trade, bequeathed 12,000 gold ducats to the Drapers' Company with the intention that the income should be used for the benefit of orphan maidens, to provide dowries 'every yere for Maydens for ever'. In subsequent years the money was put to a number of good uses which accorded with Thomas Howell's wishes; and ultimately one of the most significant schemes set up under the bequest was that which led to the foundation in 1860 of Howell's School, in the cathedral village of Llandaff. The splendid, grey stone, mid-Victorian Gothic building which is still the focal point of the School today was designed

LLANDAFF SCHOOL FIRE DAMAGE.

Classes to go on as Usual To-day.

Hundreds of sightseers made their way to Howell's School for Girls, Llandaff, Cardiff, on Sunday, but were not allowed inside the school grounds.

A *Western Mail & South Wales News* reporter gained admittance, however, and spoke to Alderman G. Fred Evans, as well as to several mistresses and the school housekeeper, Miss Holland. It was stated that school would be conducted as usual this (Monday) morning and that, apart from great inconvenience, the fire would in no way interrupt the normal course of school work.

Alderman Evans would not venture on an estimate of the extent of the damage done. He said that a meeting of the governors would be held at the school on Monday afternoon, when such details would be gone into.

Councillor C. G. Moreland was of opinion that an expenditure of several thousands of pounds will be necessary to repair the damage.

Miss Holland paid a tribute to the Cardiff Fire Brigade and said their successful efforts to save the beautiful assembly-hall, with its many treasures, were beyond praise.

by the acclaimed architect Decimus Burton. The interior of the building, as well as the exterior, attracted much favourable comment. One of its outstanding features was a beautiful assembly hall, which was almost destroyed when a fire broke out at the School on the night of Friday, 19th February, 1932. It was thought that the fire started in flues over the boilerhouse, and it spread along the roof of the east and west wings, destroying the stone hall, dining-hall and several classrooms and studies on the first floor. Fortunately the assembly hall, with its many treasures, was saved. After the fire the boarders, none of whom suffered any ill-effects, were complimented on their sensible and orderly behaviour during the evacuation; apparently the younger girls thought it all rather a lark!

In more recent years, of course, the School has been extended and modernised to provide pupils and staff with excellent facilities in all curriculum areas. It now has its own self-contained Nursery for three-year-olds, a Junior

Above: The newspaper report on the fire at the school in 1932.
Below: The school at the end of the 19th century.

from as far away as London and Brighton. The opening of the new School was, quite rightly, recognised as a tremendous opportunity for Orphans, offering them as it did clothes, board and lodging for ten months a year until they reached the age of 17, as well as providing a superior education which would equip them to earn their own livings as governesses. And while governesses have disappeared over the years, the underlying principal has not changed - pupils still leave the School equipped with all the knowledge and skills they need to succeed in their chosen career or lifestyle.

Today, girls between the age of three and 18 are admitted to the School on the basis of their academic potential and ability, without reference to religion, ethnic background or beliefs. Pupils are encouraged to be inquisitive and creative and to see learning as an exciting process, and the School's consistently outstanding examination results testify to the success of this method of teaching. Throughout the School there is a strong commitment to pastoral care, so that, during their time there, girls not only fulfill their true academic potential but also develop a sense of their own value and grow into confident and responsible members of the community. So, although the young women of the next millennium can look forward to a very different future from that of the Maydens of the 16th century, Howell's School continues to provide them with the best education, and after more than 400 years Thomas Howell's legacy remains as relevant as ever.

School - complete with its own hall, library, computer room, music room, classrooms and recreation area - for girls aged from four to eleven, and a Sixth Form Centre in its own extensive grounds with common rooms, quiet study rooms and teaching areas. There are also impressive facilities for art, craft and design, music, drama, computing and sports, together with a state-of-the-art library.

The School's first official advertisement of the availability of places for Orphans and Pay Boarders appeared in The Times in January 1860. Application forms soon began to arrive, and every application was considered carefully by the School Governors; in the case of Orphans, it had been agreed that the Governors should select the offspring 'of persons in business or offices or farms who, if they had lived, would have been able to give their children a superior education'. Among the first intake of pupils, the furthest any of the Pay Boarders had come was from Swansea, while Orphans came

Above left: *Music classes.*
Top: *An aerial view of the school.*

Cardiff made Ice Cream with a difference

The story began in 1922 when Joseph Thayer, a retired colliery overman, bought a shop in Cwm. Both he and his son, AC Thayer, built up two good general grocers in Marine Street. By 1937 Joseph Thayer was ready to retire a second time and to hand over to AC and Roy Thayer. Two years later the brothers bought, from Mrs Francis Day, a High Class Dairy and Poulterers with first refrigerated display window in Cardiff.

Cyril Thayer established pioneered the first 'self service' grocery in South Wales which became a roaring success among customers used to queuing two or three times at different counters within the same grocery shop.

Cyril Thayer noticed that many of the ices sold at a shop around the corner were being thrown away by dissatisfied customers. He tried one and decided that 'If I cannot make a better ice-cream than that, I'd eat my hat.' He spent £350, the equivalent of a year's pay packet on machinery for the job. Right away his product was so good that luxury hungry Cardiffians queued to buy his ice cream long after rationing finally finished. As the strange ingredients of post war ices were replaced by milk products the quality of Thayer's Ice Cream continued to lead the field in the Cardiff hinterland. Eventually Thayers made nothing but real Dairy Ice Cream.

During the 1950s the shops in Cwm were sold as the firm moved into Cardiff. Joseph Thayer died, followed by his wife, in 1960. In the next year Roy Thayer left the company in the hands of Mr and Mrs AC Thayer who were joined by their son DC

Thayer. Their ice cream factory was at the back of their one self service grocery when the Thayers, as usual in the know about forthcoming developments in the trade, decided to drop the grocery business. Supermarkets were making their presence felt in family run grocers around the country and the Thayers were ready to expand their growing ice cream business.

The shop premises were changed to accommodate a larger ice cream parlour and a new coffee bar. In 1963 the family bought their first ice cream Kiosk, a Turkish word for a refreshment pavilion, in Mill Lane which was added to by one on Penarth Pier. As the three retail outlets did well the Thayers planned to expand their factory until the business showed that a completely new building would be more cost effective.

By borrowing money Thayers managed to continue production and fund the new premises which had production capacity to supply thirteen wholesalers as well as their own outlets. Nowadays Thayers is in fact one of the largest producers of ice cream.

The business was finally purchased by the current owner, Robert Hodge, in 1996 after the firm had expanded its distribution countrywide. He later bought the New England Ice Cream Company and merged it with Thayers to form Thayers New England.

The tradition, cast by Cyril Thayer fifty years ago of producing high quality ice creams, still today is in the forefront of Thayers strategy and sixty people, dedicated to this objective, are employed in the Rumney site that Cyril Thayer had built.

Left: *Ice Cream production.*

The 10th of September 1947 was a day of celebration for Cardiff as John Crichton-Stuart, the 5th Marquess of Bute, presented Cardiff Castle and its grounds and Sophia Gardens to the City of Cardiff.

Acknowledgments

Cardiff County Council - Libraries and Information Division; Paul Sawyer; Geoff Rich; Bryn Jones; Alan Evans, Cardiff Rugby Club Media Officer; The Welsh Guards; Peter Harvey; Marion Wilson

Thanks are also due to Peggy Burns who penned the editorial text and Margaret Wakefield and Mike Kirke for their copywriting skills